Hope That Endures

Hope That Endures

Revelation for the Persecuted Church

BENJAMIN JOHNSON

RESOURCE *Publications* • Eugene, Oregon

HOPE THAT ENDURES
Revelation for the Persecuted Church

Copyright © 2025 Benjamin Johnson. All rights reserved. Except for brief quotations in critical publications or reviews, no part of this book may be reproduced in any manner without prior written permission from the publisher. Write: Permissions, Wipf and Stock Publishers, 199 W. 8th Ave., Suite 3, Eugene, OR 97401.

Resource Publications
An Imprint of Wipf and Stock Publishers
199 W. 8th Ave., Suite 3
Eugene, OR 97401

www.wipfandstock.com

PAPERBACK ISBN: 979-8-3852-6550-3
HARDCOVER ISBN: 979-8-3852-6551-0
EBOOK ISBN: 979-8-3852-6552-7

11/17/25

Unless otherwise noted, Scripture quotations are from the ESV® Bible (The Holy Bible, English Standard Version®), copyright © 2001 by Crossway, a publishing ministry of Good News Publishers. Used by permission. All rights reserved.

This book is dedicated to my mother, Susan Johnson, whose faithful witness led me to Christ, whose love raised me in the Lord, and whose helpful conversations strengthened this work from the very beginning.

And to my amazing wife, Patricia Hazim, who first introduced me to the deeper study of the Revelation of Jesus Christ and helped resource my understanding of its message with greater clarity.

Contents

Acknowledgments | ix
Introduction to This Commentary on Revelation | xi
Chapter One: The Revelation of Jesus Christ | 1
Chapter Two: Seven Churches Called to Endurance | 6
Chapter Three: The Lamb Alone Is Found Worthy | 12
Chapter Four: The Lamb Opens the Seals | 17
Chapter Five: The Trumpets as Wake-Up Calls | 23
Chapter Six: The Angel and the Temple of God | 29
Chapter Seven: The Two Witnesses | 34
    Excursus: The 1,260 Days—From Daniel to Revelation | 40
Chapter Eight: The Overall Biblical Story | 43
Chapter Nine: Beasts Rise | 48
    Excursus: Who Is the Antichrist? A Biblical Pattern and a Personal Future | 54
Chapter Ten: The Bowls of Wrath | 56
Chapter Eleven: Babylon Revealed | 61
Chapter Twelve: The Return and Reign of Christ | 66
Chapter Thirteen: The Release of Satan and Final Rebellion | 70
Chapter Fourteen: The New Creation | 76
Chapter Fifteen: Jesus Is Coming | 81
Epilogue: Jesus, the Morning Star | 87
    Glossary | 89
    Bibliography | 97

Acknowledgments

SPECIAL THANKS TO THE preaching team at Mill City Church, Cayce, South Carolina—whose Revelation sermon series provided clarity, encouragement, and pastoral insight that shaped portions of this work.

Special thanks to the contribution of Chet Phillips (Mill City Church, Cayce, South Carolina), who offered foundational pastoral groundwork and early guidance that sharpened the structure and clarity of this project.

Special thanks to Joe Tannous, project director at 10/40 Hope, who provided substantive review and edits that strengthened the manuscript.

I wish to acknowledge the assistance of AI-based tools, including ChatGPT, which were used at various stages of the writing process to refine wording, clarify structure, and enhance clarity.

The interpretations and applications found in this book remain the responsibility of the author. The author is thankful for these voices and the broader community of teachers and pastors who continue to equip the church to read God's word faithfully in every season—especially in suffering.

Introduction to This Commentary on Revelation

MANY CHRISTIANS AVOID THE book of Revelation because it feels mysterious, confusing, or only about the distant future. But Revelation was written, not as a puzzle to decode, but as a vision of Jesus meant to give hope, courage, and clarity to everyday believers. It shows us how to live faithfully in a world that often feels like it's shaking apart. This book is especially written for Christians in America who may not face physical persecution like many do around the world, but who still experience pressure, fear, and cultural confusion. We face different kinds of trials—moral compromise, cultural chaos, political upheaval, and uncertainty about the future. Revelation speaks directly into that. It shows us that Jesus is alive, reigning, and with his people—no matter what happens in the world.

Throughout this commentary, you'll find simple explanations, engaging reflections, and practical takeaways. Each section begins with a short overview of what John saw and closes with why it still matters today. Discussion questions at the end of each chapter help you apply the message to your own life, family, and church. Above all, this book will help you see Revelation, not as an escape plan, but as a call to courageous discipleship. When everything feels uncertain, the throne of heaven is not. Jesus reigns, his victory is secure, and his people are called to endure with faith and hope until the day he returns.

This commentary seeks to offer a clear and faithful interpretation of Revelation, honoring its original context, theological

Introduction to This Commentary on Revelation

depth, and relevance for today. At its core, Revelation calls the church to remain faithful to Jesus in the face of pressure, persecution, and deception. It reveals Jesus Christ as the risen King who rules now and who will return to fully establish his kingdom on earth. Revelation assures us that despite appearances, evil will not have the final word—God will.

From the very beginning, the purpose of Revelation is made clear. In Rev 1:19, John is told, "Write therefore the things that you have seen, those that are and those that are to take place after this." This divine instruction helps us understand that Revelation includes past, present, and future realities. It was immediately relevant to the churches of John's day, speaking directly to their struggles and trials. At the same time, it unveils God's ongoing work throughout history and points forward to the ultimate fulfillment of his redemptive plan.

Throughout history, sincere Christians have tried to understand Revelation through different lenses: the preterist, which sees much of the book fulfilled in the early church; the futurist, which focuses on Christ's future return and judgment; the historicist, which traces its fulfillment across the broad span of church history; and the idealist, which views it as symbolic of timeless spiritual truths. While this commentary acknowledges all four frameworks, it doesn't follow any of them rigidly. Instead, it draws from the strengths of each. Like the preterist, it takes seriously the historical context and first-century relevance. Like the futurist, it affirms that Revelation speaks of Christ's return and final judgment. From the historicist, it recognizes the long sweep of redemptive history and the recurring patterns of persecution and endurance. And from the idealist, it values the spiritual truths and symbolic depth that transcend any single moment in time. Rather than forcing Revelation into a single mold, this commentary integrates these perspectives where they are most helpful—and sets aside the extremes and blind spots of each.

At the beginning of each chapter, a short overview of the vision will be provided. Readers are encouraged to read the biblical passage(s) referenced before engaging with the commentary, so

Introduction to This Commentary on Revelation

that the details remain fresh in mind. This ensures that the text of Scripture—not interpretation—shapes understanding. Extended Scripture quotations are not included in the body of the text; readers should consult their own Bible when directed. Short phrases or references may appear for clarity.

As one moves through Revelation, the goal is not only to interpret symbols but to hear what the Spirit is saying to the church today. Readers do not need to be scholars to benefit—only followers of Jesus who long to remain faithful, no matter the cost. Above all, Revelation is a call to endurance. Not endurance that merely waits for escape, but endurance that keeps standing, keeps worshiping, and keeps resisting compromise, even when it costs everything. Revelation is not escapism—it is discipleship for a persecuted church.

Tribulation is real—but so is the kingdom. Revelation places both realities side by side: while the saints suffer (Rev 13), the Lamb still reigns (Rev 14). The Lamb who was slain now stands in the center of heaven, surrounded by worship. The scroll of history is in his hand. The seals will be broken. Judgment will fall. And yet the church remains, called to be faithful witnesses no matter what beast rises or what empire collapses. The world may look like chaos, but the throne is still occupied. Revelation reminds us that we are not waiting for hope—we are already walking in it. The victory has been won. The return is coming. And in the meantime, the church is called to hold fast, to see clearly, to worship boldly, and to endure joyfully. This is a book for the church in every age. And it is a book for right now.

About "The Word of Their Testimony"

At the end of several chapters, you'll find real-life stories of ordinary believers walking in extraordinary endurance, faith, and obedience. These aren't illustrations, they are witnesses. They reflect what Revelation says about those who overcome: "By the blood of the Lamb and the word of their testimony" (Rev 12:11).

Introduction to This Commentary on Revelation

These stories come from believers living in what is often called the 10/40 Window—a region stretching across North Africa, the Middle East, and Asia, where billions of people live with little access to the gospel and where following Jesus often comes with great risk.

The names and locations have been withheld for security, but the stories are real. They remind us that the message of Revelation isn't ancient history or future prediction—it's happening now. The church is alive, the Lamb is reigning, and faithful witnesses are still standing in the fire.

Myth vs. Truth

Myth: Revelation is mainly about predicting dates.

Truth: Revelation is about living faithfully in the present.

Myth: Revelation is a scary codebook for end times.

Truth: Revelation is a hopeful vision of Jesus, written to encourage the church.

Myth: Revelation doesn't apply to us today.

Truth: Every message was written for the church in every age—including ours.

CHAPTER ONE

The Revelation of Jesus Christ

What John Sees

JOHN, EXILED ON PATMOS, is caught up in the Spirit and sees the risen Christ walking among the seven lampstands. Jesus reveals his divine titles, reassures John, and commissions him to write to the churches. The seven stars and seven lampstands are explained, anchoring the whole book in Jesus's living presence with his people.

Reference: Revelation chapter 1

The Purpose of the Revelation

Revelation begins with clarity and urgency. This is not a riddle or a theological game—it is a revelation. God is not trying to confuse his people; he's revealing something they need to know. Specifically, it is the revelation of Jesus Christ, given by the Father, delivered through an angel, entrusted to John, and meant for the church. From the very first sentence, the reader is reminded that this book is about Jesus. His nature. His authority. His return. His reign.

Verse 1 introduces a dual emphasis: the urgency of what is revealed, and its divine origin. While the phrase "shortly take place" does not specify exact timing, it does convey that the unfolding of these events is imminent from God's perspective.

John records what he sees and hears in the Spirit. Sometimes the meaning of the signs and symbols is explained directly; at other times, the reader must rely on the context familiar to John's original audience. They did not know exactly how events would unfold, yet they recognized the significance of what was being communicated. Though Revelation speaks in symbols, its purpose is to reveal, not to conceal.

This revelation is for "his servants." It is not secret knowledge for spiritual elites but is meant to be heard aloud, understood, and obeyed by everyday believers. It carries a blessing—not only for those who study it but also for those who keep it. Revelation is written not merely to inform the church but to strengthen and steady it, for the time, as John writes, is near.

This message is addressed to seven churches in modern-day Turkey in the first century—real churches, facing real pressure. However, the number seven also signals something deeper. Since John receives the Revelation as apocalyptic (see glossary) imagery, its numbers often carry both symbolic meaning and historical reference (Zech 1:18–21; Ezek 47:1–12). In Scripture, seven represents fullness or completeness. These churches serve as a symbolic representation of the whole church across time and geography. What Jesus says to them, he says to all the churches until his return.

Here we see God, who is one yet revealed in three. The Father who always was and will be. The Holy Spirit is described as "the seven spirits before God's throne" (Rev 1:4). This phrase is most likely a reference to a passage in Isa 11:2, which describes the Spirit of the Lord in seven ways: the Spirit of the Lord, wisdom, understanding, counsel, might, knowledge, and the fear of the Lord.

These aren't separate spirits—they're different aspects of the Holy Spirit's work. This number communicates that he is fully complete and perfectly present. Together, these attributes describe the Spirit's role in giving strength, guidance, and wisdom to God's people.

Jesus is then described in three ways: as the faithful witness, firstborn from the dead, and ruler of kings on earth. In other words, he has spoken the truth, conquered the grave, and now reigns over every power—no matter what it looks like. To this King, John says, belongs all glory and dominion. No good and faithful Jew would say this of any man, so John makes sure his readers understand that Jesus is God the Son.

Jesus is not a quiet figure from history. He's alive, in charge, and present with his people. When John sees him, he falls in fear—but Jesus reaches out, touches him, and says, "Don't be afraid" (Rev 1:17). This moment shows Jesus as powerful and kind, full of strength and compassion.

He says he's the First and the Last, the One who died and came back to life. He holds the keys to death and all authority. This isn't just a spiritual idea; it's a real reason to hope.

Now John speaks—not as an apostle demanding authority, but as a brother and partner in the struggle. John says in Rev 1:9, "I, John, your brother and partner in the tribulation and the kingdom and the patient endurance that are in Jesus, was on the island called Patmos on account of the word of God and the testimony of Jesus." This matters. He doesn't write Revelation from a place of comfort, but from the island of Patmos, where he has been exiled for preaching the word of God and bearing witness to Jesus. His suffering is not allegorical but literal, reminding the reader that tribulation is not reserved for a future generation—it is the ongoing reality of faithful believers in a hostile world. The Greek word *thlipsis*, translated as "tribulation," conveys the sense of crushing pressure.[1] That pressure is what Christians often experience when they resist the compromises of a culture opposed to Christ.[2]

John names three things all believers share: tribulation, the kingdom, and patient endurance. These are not separate phases or stages. They're all part of what it means to belong to Jesus in a hostile world. Revelation begins by anchoring us here: in real suffering, waiting for a real kingdom, calling for real perseverance.

1. Bible Hub, "2347. thlipsis."
2. Keener, *Revelation*, 81–82. Craig Keener's commentary significantly shaped my understanding of Revelation and helped set me on this journey of studying it more deeply. I found his work especially helpful in framing my understanding of the messages to the churches, the seals, the trumpets, the two witnesses, Babylon, and the antichrist.

Revelation, therefore, is not primarily about escape from tribulation, but about perseverance through it. It offers hope to the church during spiritual conflict—not a conflict against flesh and blood, but against spiritual forces, worldly systems, and the constant temptation to abandon faithfulness.

John is worshipping the Lord on Sunday when the vision begins. A loud voice like a trumpet breaks through the silence—sharp, commanding, unmistakable. The instruction is clear: write what you see and send it to the churches. This isn't private revelation. This is a word for the whole church, then and now.

When John turns, he sees Jesus—not standing above the churches, not watching from a safe distance, but amid the lampstands. John is told the lampstands represent the churches (v. 20). This is the central image of chapter one: Jesus is present with his people. Right there in the middle of their pressure, pain, and faithfulness.

The vision is overwhelming. Jesus appears in radiant, terrifying glory. He is ancient, wise, all-seeing, unstoppable. His words cut through illusion and lie. His voice shakes the earth. His face blazes like the sun. This is the risen Christ—not reduced, not vague, not merely historical. He is alive and blazing with divine majesty.

And he holds seven stars in his right hand. These stars, John is told, are "the angels [messengers] of the seven churches"—whether symbolic of spiritual beings or human leaders, the point is clear: Jesus holds them and the churches they represent securely in his grip.

John's response is a total collapse. But Jesus reaches out. The same hand that holds the stars now touches a trembling servant. "Fear not." That's the heart of this entire book. Jesus is not just terrifying in power—he is tender in love. He says, "I died, and now I live forever. And I hold the keys." That's real authority—not just over nations, but over death itself.

Jesus repeats the commission: write what you've seen, what is, and what will be. This is the divine outline of Revelation—past vision, present condition, and future fulfillment.

The Revelation of Jesus Christ
Why It Still Matters Today

This is how Revelation begins—not with fear, but with presence. Jesus is alive. Jesus is with us. Jesus sees everything, holds everything, and reigns over everything. And in a world full of shaking ground and spiritual compromise, this vision calls the church to endure with confidence no matter what we may face. The message is crystal clear: before we get to judgment, dragons, or victory, we get this—Jesus, with his church, full of glory and full of grace.

The Word of Their Testimony

A man reached out after seeing an ad from an online ministry. He said Jesus had appeared to him in a dream and asked, "Why did this happen to me?" He was met with care, answers, and truth over Zoom. He gave his life to Christ in a nation where you can be arrested for converting. When Jesus seeks someone, he finds them—and they find him.

Questions for Reflection and Discussion

- Why is it significant that John opens the book and greets the church as their brother in the tribulation?
- What is significant about Jesus's appearance when John sees him?

CHAPTER TWO

Seven Churches Called to Endurance

What John Sees

JOHN SEES SEVEN LAMPSTANDS, which are revealed as churches. Jesus addresses them—affirming faithfulness, correcting compromise, and calling for endurance. Each message reveals what Christ values in his church and promises reward to those who overcome.
Reference: Revelation chapters 2–3

Jesus Is the Shepherd of His Church

These seven churches that Jesus will address represent the full range of what churches can become: vibrant or dead, faithful or compromised, courageous or comfortable. Jesus walks among them. He knows what's going on inside each one, not just what people see from the outside. He addresses what's healthy, what's broken, and what needs to change. He doesn't speak in generalities. He speaks with specificity, with urgency, and with love. He affirms. He corrects. He promises. And in every message, he calls the church to overcome and endure.

Seven Churches Called to Endurance

Ephesus: Truth Without Love

Ephesus was a hub of commerce and pagan worship, home to the temple of Artemis, one of the wonders of the ancient world. Into this city the gospel came, and a church was planted. The believers persevered through hardship, resisted false apostles, and endured for Christ's name—yet they abandoned the love they had at first. The church could recognize error, but its passion for Christ and his people was fading.

The warning is sobering even now: a church may be active, doctrinally sound, and outwardly respected, yet hollow within. Jesus is not satisfied with outward obedience alone—he desires hearts and compassion.[1]

Smyrna: Suffering with Nothing to Hide

Smyrna was a proud and wealthy city, fiercely loyal to Rome. It was a center of emperor worship, and Christians who refused to participate were excluded, slandered, and persecuted for their faith. But Jesus told them the truth: "You are rich" (2:9). Their reward would not be found in Roman approval or earthly status, but in a Savior who conquered death.

Jesus also told them they would face "ten days of testing" (v. 10). For the believers in Smyrna, this most likely referred to a literal, short period of intense persecution. The phrase would have been vivid and concrete to them: literal days they could count, an ordeal with a clear beginning and end.

At the same time, throughout Scripture, the number ten often points to completeness in human experience or responsibility before God—such as the Ten Commandments (Exod 20), the ten plagues (Exod 7–12), or Daniel's ten-day test in Babylon (Dan 1:12–14). Here, it signified that their time of testing would be a set time but limited by God's sovereignty. Revelation often weaves together the concrete and the symbolic to reassure the church: their

---

1. Keener, *Revelation*, 106.

suffering was real, but it was defined, measured, and would not last beyond what God allowed.

For the original audience, these words from the risen Christ anchored their identity. When Jesus said, "Be faithful unto death" (2:10), he was not being poetic—some of them would literally die. Yet death was not the end; it was the doorway. The same is true today. Christians facing persecution around the world are not forgotten. And when we face trials, even small ones, we remember faithfulness always matters more than comfort.[2]

Pergamum: Faithful but Flirting with Compromise

Pergamum was a hub of idolatry, imperial cult worship, and pressure to conform. Jesus praises the believers for their bold stand. They stay loyal in a place Jesus calls "Satan's throne" (v. 13), most likely a reference to the large temple of Zeus located in the city.[3] That language would've hit hard—this was not neutral territory. However, even courageous churches are vulnerable. False teaching had crept in—compromising teaching that mixed the gospel with idolatry and immorality. The references to Balaam and the Nicolaitans weren't abstract; they pointed to people within the church who were trying to blend faith with culture.

To the original audience, this wasn't academic. It was survival. And Jesus makes it clear: loyalty means more than standing firm in public—it means guarding the truth in private. Today, this is applied by asking, Where has truth been softened for the sake of comfort? Where is sin left tolerated and unconfronted in the lives of his people?

Thyatira: Love Grows but So Does Tolerance for Sin

Thyatira was known for trade unions and economic power, and participation in those associations often meant taking part in

---

2. Keener, *Revelation*, 116.
3. Keener, *Revelation*, 123.

pagan feasts and idol worship. For the church there, compromise often came wrapped in pressure to keep a job and provide for one's family. The woman referred to as "Jezebel" (v. 20) may have been a real leader in the church, or a symbolic reference to a corrupting influence that encouraged spiritual and moral compromise under the guise of Christian liberty.

To the original hearers, Jesus's message was direct: love and growth are good, but not if they come at the expense of holiness. Not all tolerance is a virtue. Today, when churches celebrate love and inclusion while ignoring sin, the message of Thyatira confronts us. Jesus doesn't just affirm growth—he demands purity. But his tone is still merciful: "I gave her time to repent" (v. 21). His patience is real, but so is his judgment. He promises to give them the morning star if they overcome. The significance of this reward will be revealed to them later in the revelation.[4]

Sardis: Wake Up Before It's Too Late

Sardis had a reputation for wealth and prestige. The church in Sardis looked alive from the outside. Their reputation was strong—but their spiritual life was fading. Jesus saw through it all. This was not just spiritual decline; it was spiritual apathy. He called them to wake up and return to what they had once known.

The urgency here is sharp. Jesus is not warning of casual consequences—he says, "I will come like a thief" (3:3). It is a warning of judgment. Yet even in this sobering message, there is hope. A few remained faithful, and to them Jesus promised white garments and their names confessed before the Father. For today's church, the lesson is clear: image is not enough. Reputation means nothing without genuine faith. Jesus calls us to a life of substance, not appearances.[5]

---

4. Keener, *Revelation*, 133–36.
5. Keener, *Revelation*, 144.

Hope That Endures

Philadelphia: Faithful with Little Strength

The church in Philadelphia was not powerful, but it was faithful. Jesus knows they "have little strength" (v. 8), yet he honors their endurance. He sets before them an "open door—a door no one can shut."

For the original audience, this was reassurance: they did not need status to be used by God. What mattered was faithfulness. And to this small, unimpressive church, Jesus gives some of his greatest promises—protection in trial, permanence in God's presence, and a new name that reflects their eternal identity. For today, especially those who feel weak or overlooked, this message is deeply encouraging. Jesus notices the faithful, and he will reward them.

Laodicea: Deceived by Prosperity

Laodicea was a wealthy city, known for its banking, textiles, and medicine.[6] But the church had absorbed the spirit of its culture—comfortable, self-reliant, and blind to its real condition. Jesus told them the truth: "You think you have everything, but you have nothing."

This is the only letter where Jesus offers no praise. But even here, his tone is love. "Those whom I love, I reprove and discipline" (v. 19). He's knocking—not to condemn, but to restore. The promise is intimate: he wants to come in and fellowship with them.

To the church today, this is a crucial warning. Comfort can dull spiritual senses. Prosperity can blind us to our true needs. Jesus is not impressed with outward wealth—he's looking for faithfulness and passionate devotion. And even when his people drift, he still pursues them, but he won't settle for lukewarm.

---

6. Keener, *Revelation*, 160.

Seven Churches Called to Endurance
Why It Still Matters Today

These messages are not random. They're not ancient history. They are a mirror. Jesus speaks to churches with clarity and conviction because he wants them alive, pure, and ready. Each message carried real-time implications for the churches that first received it. The way the church can arrive at application today is by recognizing the same spiritual dynamics in its own context. Pressure. Compromise. Fatigue. Drift. The forms may change, but the call is the same: stay faithful and endure!

He's still speaking. And the church still needs to listen. Let the one who has ears hear what the Spirit is saying to the churches.

Questions for Reflection and Discussion

- How does Jesus's closeness to his church change how you view challenging times?
- How can you help others see that suffering doesn't mean failure; it can be a sign of faithfulness?
- As you read Christ's words to the seven churches, which one most closely resembles your own church's strengths and struggles?

CHAPTER THREE

The Lamb Alone Is Found Worthy

What John Sees

Heaven opens to the throne room where unending worship centers on God and the Lamb. The Lamb alone is worthy to take the scroll and open its seals; history moves under his authority.
 Reference: Revelation chapters 4–5

Heaven Is Revealed

This moment marks a transition in the book's structure. The preceding chapters contain letters to seven churches, addressing the present condition of the church in John's time, what may be called "the things that are." But Rev 4:1 introduces "the things that will take place after this," signaling a shift into the prophetic vision of what lies ahead.

John is taken up into the spiritual realm and given a vision of God's throne room—much like what Isa 6:1–5; Ezek 1:1–28; and 10:1–22 described centuries earlier. John is overwhelmed as his eyes are drawn to the living creatures surrounding the throne, who never cease crying out, "Holy, holy, holy, is the Lord God Almighty, who was and is and is to come!" (Rev 4:8). These exalted beings—whose very presence would terrify mortals—cannot tear

The Lamb Alone Is Found Worthy

their gaze away from the One seated on the throne. Their unending worship declares that God is utterly set apart—unique in his being, unmatched in his power, and without rival in all creation. The elders join them, casting their crowns before him, for even their heavenly authority pales before his glory. The scene makes one truth unmistakable: the closer one comes to God's presence, the clearer it becomes that there is nothing and no one in all the universe that compares to him.

The message this vision communicates is also clear—before anything happens on earth, heaven is not in panic. God is on the throne, sovereign and unshaken.

Then the spotlight shifts. In God's right hand is a scroll, sealed with seven seals. Scrolls represented the sovereign plans of kings throughout history. Here, contained in this scroll, are God's decrees for justice, judgment, redemption, and the end of history itself. This would become clear to John's audience as they would continue to read this Revelation.

Here, a crisis emerges: no one in heaven or on earth is found worthy to open the scroll or even look at it. No spiritual being, no prophet, no ruler is qualified. And so, John begins to weep. This weeping is not just emotional—it is theological. John feels crushed by the possibility that God's purposes might remain sealed. If the scroll is not opened, evil goes unpunished, injustice continues, and hope is deferred. John's tears are the tears of the persecuted church.

John then hears one of the elders tell him, "Stop weeping. Look! The Lion of the tribe of Judah, the Root of David, has triumphed. He is able to open the scroll" (5:5). This announcement is loaded with messianic power. The Lion of Judah is a title steeped in Old Testament imagery, evoking strength, royalty, and conquest—the kind of Messiah many Jews expected: a fierce, victorious king who would crush his enemies and restore Israel's glory. It's a declaration of triumph. But when John turns to look, he doesn't see a lion. Instead, he sees a Lamb, not just gentle but "looking as if it had been slain" (v. 6). It's a shocking reversal. The conquering king isn't a tyrant, but a leader who gives his life for his subjects. The victory hasn't come through force or violence, but through suffering and death. Power, in Revelation, is redefined through the cross.

This moment sets a critical pattern for the rest of the book: what John hears and what he sees are often in tension, and that tension is theologically rich. He hears "lion"—a symbol of dominance—but sees "lamb"—a symbol of self-giving love. The Lion has conquered because he is the slain Lamb. This becomes the lens through which all Revelation should be read.

John will experience this hear-see contrast throughout the Revelation: this pattern is not just literary—it's prophetic. It calls the reader to look deeper, to question assumptions about power, victory, and God's way of working in the world.

This is the turning point. Jesus, the Lamb who was slain, is both the conquering King and the suffering Servant. He alone is worthy to open the scroll because he conquered through sacrifice. He did not defeat evil by force but by laying down his life. This is the paradox of the gospel: the cross is the place of victory. His wounds are his credentials. And through his blood, he ransomed people for God from every tribe, language, people, and nation.

The opening of the scroll is not just the beginning of the end—it is the assurance that history is not stuck, that God's justice is coming, and that redemption will be complete. And at the center of it all stands the Lamb—worthy, reigning, and leading his people through suffering into glory. He alone carries the authority to unleash what comes next. This vision prepares the reader for the seals, but more than that, it centers them. The Lamb is leading history.

Why It Still Matters Today

This vision was first given to anchor persecuted believers in the first century, yet it continues to anchor us today. When life feels chaotic, when injustice goes unchecked, and when the church suffers under pressure, Revelation points us to three unshakable truths.

The Lamb Alone Is Found Worthy

First, the throne is occupied. Heaven is never in crisis. God rules, unshaken by the rise and fall of empires or the turmoil of our age. Every headline that threatens to overwhelm us remains firmly beneath his authority.

Second, the Lamb leads history. The one who directs the unfolding of God's plan is not a distant ruler or a harsh tyrant but the Lamb who bore our sins. His wounds assure us that the one guiding history's course is also the one who loves us to the uttermost, having given his life for us.

Third, the scroll will be opened. The purposes of God will not remain sealed forever. Justice will be done. Redemption will be completed. The end of the story is not uncertain—it is already secured by the authority of the Lamb.

For those who suffer for their faith, this vision lifts our eyes from the shaking of earth to the stability of heaven. It calls us to worship rather than despair, to endure rather than lose heart, and to trust that the same Lamb who redeemed us will also bring history to its rightful conclusion. Revelation isn't just about what's going to happen; it's about how we interpret what we think we see—and about letting the Lamb reshape our understanding of reality.

When we remember that the throne is not empty and the Lamb is worthy, we can face persecution, uncertainty, and even death with unshakable hope. Heaven has been revealed, and that vision strengthens us to live faithfully on earth until the Lamb who was slain returns.

The Word of Their Testimony

A leader and his group were meeting in the woods due to safety concerns when it began to rain. They found shelter and ended up sharing space with a man gathering sticks for a fire. He said he wasn't religious, but agreed to sit in the meeting. The leader asked for his input throughout—and he responded honestly. By the end, two fishermen joined, one of whom committed to continuing to meet with the man. Everyone in the group realized that the rain had simply rerouted them—for the sake of one soul. God's hand can be hidden in the inconvenience. When his people move forward in faith, he brings divine appointments in unlikely places.

Questions for Reflection and Discussion

- John's vision begins with a door standing open in heaven and a throne that is never empty. How does remembering that God's throne is occupied change the way we respond to chaos or suffering in our world today?
- John wept when no one was found worthy of opening the scroll. In what ways do we share that same longing for God to intervene, bring justice, and make things right?
- John heard about a conquering Lion but saw a slain Lamb. What does this paradox teach us about the nature of Jesus's victory and how God's power often appears different from our expectations?
- Revelation shows that the one guiding the course of history bears the wounds of sacrifice. How does this truth encourage you to trust Christ's leadership in your own life and in the larger story of the world?

CHAPTER FOUR

The Lamb Opens the Seals

What John Sees

THE LAMB OPENS SIX seals, unveiling conquest, violence, famine, and death—unfolding God's sovereign judgment on a rebellious world. Cosmic upheaval follows, striking fear in every heart. Yet before the final seal breaks, God marks his servants for protection, and John sees a countless multitude from every nation: redeemed, secure, and worshiping before the throne.

Reference: Revelation chapters 6–7

The Seals Are Opened

As the Lamb begins to open the seals, a series of judgments are unleashed—not as random disasters, but as part of God's sovereign plan playing out across human history. These seals represent events unfolding between Christ's ascension and his return, as will be discussed later on in this book. Each is initiated at a particular moment, though the exact timing is not revealed. Once set in motion, their effects persist and reappear throughout history. War, famine, death, and the persecution of God's people aren't just future threats—they are present realities. For many believers, especially in persecuted regions, these aren't mere symbols. They are daily life.[1]

Each of the first five seals represents an aspect of divine judgment already active in the world. These judgments don't just reveal the consequences of sin—they also serve a divine purpose. They expose the rebellion of the world, test and refine the faith of God's people, and prepare creation for its final renewal. God is not absent in suffering. The Lamb himself is the one opening the seals. He is not only in control—he is present in the pain, and his plan is moving forward, even when history feels like it's unraveling.

With the first seal, we witness the rise of conquest. A rider on a white horse, crowned, charging forth. He represents the aggressive advance of worldly dominion—ambition, empire, control. It's conquest without compassion.

This is what the church has seen since the earliest days—power-hungry rulers, oppressive regimes, the seduction of control. The Lamb breaks the seal, but the judgment is not disconnected from human sin. The conquering spirit of this world plays right into the consequences God has already determined. And the church watches it unfold—not with fear, but with the clarity that heaven gave John: the Lamb is still in charge.

When the Lamb opens the second seal, the next living creature calls out with the same thunderous voice: "Come!" (6:3). And another horse appears, this one bright red. Its rider is permitted to take peace from the earth so that people begin to kill one another, and he is given a great sword. This is not just the violence of war—it's the tearing apart of human relationships. It's hostility, bloodshed, and division that spreads like wildfire. We see it all around us: civil wars, terrorism, conflict in the streets, even hatred in our own communities. This seal reminds us that when peace is removed, chaos fills the gap. The Lamb is the one opening the seal, but the violence we see is humanity's own path playing out under God's judgment. Even here, the church watches, not without grief, but with faith in the One who holds the scroll.

---

1. Keener, *Revelation*, 199–205.

The Lamb Opens the Seals

The third seal brings a black horse, and its rider carries a pair of scales. Then a voice speaks—one that seems to come from among the living creatures—saying, "A quart of wheat for a denarius, and three quarts of barley for a denarius, and do not harm the oil and wine!" (v. 6). This is the language of famine. The prices are inflated—food costs a day's wages—yet the luxuries are untouched. It's a picture of economic imbalance, where the poor suffer and the rich stay protected. Again, the judgment is not arbitrary. It reflects the injustice built into the system—exploitation, hoarding, and indifference to suffering. The black horse rides through every society that puts profit over people. And as the church witnesses it unfold, we are reminded: this isn't outside God's view. The Lamb has opened the seal. He is not distant from our need—he is present in the scarcity, working even through hardship.

With the fourth seal comes the pale horse. This one is different. Its rider is named Death, and Hades follows close behind. They are given authority over a fourth of the earth—to kill by sword, famine, pestilence, and wild beasts. It's a grim scene, and it's meant to be. This is the cumulative result of all the brokenness that came before: conquest, war, injustice—they all lead here. Death moves through the world in many forms, and Hades collects what remains. But notice this: their power is limited. A fourth of the earth, no more. Even in judgment, God sets boundaries. Death is not in charge; God is. The Lamb breaks the seal, and the rider rides out, but only within the limits heaven allows. For the church, this is not just a warning—it's a call to trust. Even death itself is under the authority of the Lamb who holds the scroll.

When the Lamb opens the fifth seal, John sees under the altar the souls of those slain for the word of God and the witness they bore. They cry out with loud voices: "O Sovereign Lord, holy and true, how long before you will judge and avenge our blood on those who live on the earth?" (v. 10). And then each of them is given a white robe and told to rest a little longer, until the number of their fellow servants and brothers who are to be killed just as they were is complete. This is not merely a vision—it is the faithful suffering of martyrs. Their cry is raw grief and urgency, yet behind it lives patience and hope. The Lamb hears their voice. He clothes them in white, gives them rest, and holds them with the promise of justice yet to come.

When the Lamb opens the sixth seal, the tone shifts dramatically. Cosmic signs shake the created order: the sun turns black, the moon becomes like blood, and the stars fall from the sky. The powerful—kings, generals, and the rich—flee in terror, as every foundation people trust in collapses. This scene echoes the language of the Old Testament prophets and even Jesus's own words when his disciples asked about the end of the age (Matt 24). In the midst of the chaos, a piercing question rises: "Who can stand in the day of God's wrath?" (Rev 6:17). This is more than a cry of fear—it is a deeply theological question. When judgment comes, who will endure? Who has a foundation that cannot be shaken?

John Hears a Number, but Sees a Multitude

Then John hears the number of those sealed: 144,000 from the tribes of Israel (7:4). This number is symbolic—twelve tribes multiplied and squared, signifying the fullness of God's people. It does not point to ethnicity or a literal head count but to completeness. These are the redeemed, marked by God as his own.[2] After hearing the number, John then sees a vast multitude that no one can count, from every tribe, language, people, and nation. They stand before the throne and the Lamb, clothed in white robes, holding palm branches—symbols of victory and peace. This is not the first time John has heard one thing but seen something else. Earlier he heard "the lion of the tribe of Judah," but he turned and saw a "lamb that had been slain."

These are not two separate groups. They are one church seen from two angles: the 144,000 portrays God's people on earth—sealed, secure, and protected spiritually. The great multitude shows some of the same people in glory—having come through

---

2. Keener, *Revelation*, 230–33.

The Lamb Opens the Seals

the tribulation, now worshiping in the presence of the Lamb, waiting for their brothers and sisters.[3]

This is the church universal: Jew and gentile, from all nations, saved by grace and sealed by the Spirit. The original readers in the seven churches would not have missed the significance of the number John heard and the vision he saw, especially as it comes in answer to the question, "Who can stand in the day of the Lord's wrath?" They would have understood it as applying to themselves in their tribulation with John, as well as to all believers in generations to come.

Why It Still Matters Today

Revelation is clear: God's people are not exempt from suffering. The seal does not mean escape from tribulation—but preservation through it. God knows those who are his. His mark is on them—not to remove them from harm's way, but to keep them faithful and unshaken, even as the world trembles.

This vision is not just theology—it's hope. For the persecuted and suffering church, this chapter is a lifeline. It declares that the pressures of history, the threats of persecution, and the schemes of evil cannot erase the identity of God's people. They are known, and they will stand. For they are sealed by the Lamb.

The Word of Their Testimony

One brother was leading a small group gathering in a spiritually resistant area. After the meeting, he left the house—only to be surrounded by a crowd of around twenty men. They began to beat him violently. His mother-in-law, who was with him, screamed and begged them to stop.

He was hospitalized. But by God's mercy, his injuries were only bruises. No bones were broken. No internal damage. Just pain. Just a body marked by the cost of witness. The message of

---

3. Keener, *Revelation*, 243–45.

Revelation tells us the saints are not spared from suffering—but they are never abandoned. God protects the soul, even when the body may be beaten.

Questions for Reflection and Discussion

- How should we understand the church's suffering in light of the seals?
- What does it mean that the church is "sealed"?
- How can we lead people to stand firm and turn to God while there is still time?
- When the Bible describes the sun darkening, the moon turning to blood, the stars falling, and the heavens shaking (see Isa 13:9–14; Joel 2:28–31; Matt 24; and Rev 6:12–17), what do you notice about the historical events these words were connected to?
- How might that suggest this cosmic sign language is a prophetic idiom—a way of describing God's world-shaking judgment—and that the events it points to may unfold over a period of time rather than in a single instant?

CHAPTER FIVE

The Trumpets as Wake-Up Calls

What John Sees

SILENCE IN HEAVEN PRECEDES the trumpet judgments. Incense mingles with the saints' prayers; then partial judgments (by thirds) fall, warning the world and urging repentance while preserving God's people.

Reference: Revelation chapters 8–9

The Seventh Seal

When the seventh seal is opened, there is silence in heaven for about half an hour. This pause is dramatic and intentional. After scenes of thunder, lightning, and worship, the stillness highlights the weight of what's about to unfold. It is the calm before another storm of divine judgment. The seventh seal doesn't conclude the judgments—it introduces the next stage, like a Russian nesting doll, where each layer reveals another inside.

To John's audience, this silence signifies a breathless anticipation, a moment of sacred suspense before God's response to their prayers. The incense rising with the saints' prayers connects heaven to earth. The fire hurled to the earth demonstrates that God hears and acts. For persecuted believers under Roman rule, this symbolized divine intervention at last.

The opening of the sixth and seventh seals marks the beginning of the end. These seals do not close the story but open the way for what follows. When the seventh seal is broken, seven angels are given seven trumpets, each blast introducing a new stage of God's judgment. The trumpets do not represent random disasters but an intentional escalation—each one intensifying the severity of events upon the earth. They build like the growing peals of thunder before a storm, moving history closer and closer to its climax.

In biblical tradition, trumpets are not merely sounds—they are divine signals. They have always marked decisive moments: calling God's people to battle (Num 10:9), summoning them to worship (2 Chr 5:12–13), or warning them to repent (Joel 2:1). In Revelation, the trumpets carry all three roles at once. They summon humanity to recognize God's authority, they shake the created world to its core, and they warn of the judgment that lies ahead.

It is important to notice, however, that Scripture does not tell us how many years these events cover. Some have tried to calculate exact timelines, often because of misinterpretations of the book of Daniel, but Scripture itself does not give one. The emphasis in Revelation is not on predicting dates but on hearing the warning. The escalating sequence of the trumpets shows that judgment is certain and intensifying, but the times and seasons remain in God's hands. Readers are therefore called not to speculation but to readiness, repentance, and faithfulness. They are called to endure.

Each trumpet brings increasing severity, but the judgments are partial, affecting one-third of creation. This limited scope reveals God's mercy even in judgment. His purpose is not total destruction, but to call people to repentance before it's too late.

Trumpets One Through Four: Judgment on the Natural World

The trumpets in Revelation are not wild chaos; they are purposeful, measured, and divine. God restrains their force to give room for

The Trumpets as Wake-Up Calls

repentance. Each trumpet is a wake-up call. But the deeper danger lies, not in the plagues, but in the hearts that refuse to listen.

These first four trumpets affect the created order—earth, sea, fresh water, and sky. But each is restrained. Only a third is struck. Even in judgment, God limits the devastation, allowing room for repentance. These are warning signs, not final blows.

To John's first-century readers, the imagery of fire, blood, poisoned water, and darkened skies would have evoked memories of the exodus plagues. It would have reminded them that just as God judged Egypt and rescued his people, he would judge the wicked and deliver them as well. It would also bring fear to those still tied to the Roman system, symbolized by ships and sea commerce.

The cry from the eagle prepares the reader for what's next. The final three trumpets—called "woes"—are more direct. They will strike humanity, not just the environment.

Trumpets Five Through Seven: Judgment on Humanity

The fifth trumpet unleashes a terrifying plague—not natural, but supernatural. Demonic tormentors emerge from the abyss, targeting only the unsealed, those without God's protection. Their purpose is not to kill but to afflict. Even in wrath, the intent is to awaken. The vivid description of these locusts underscores their unnatural origin. They are creatures of judgment, agents of torment. Their king—named Destroyer—rules over the abyss, but only by permission. For John's audience, this is a reversal of the imperial promise of peace. Rome cannot protect them from these forces. Only the seal of God matters. The seal does not mean God's people will not endure suffering, but God knows who his are, and they are eternally secure in him.

The sixth trumpet—the second woe—goes further than torment. Death returns. Four angels, long restrained, are now loose, and what follows is not random destruction, but judgment at an exact, appointed time. Here, judgment intensifies. The imagery is warlike, but the scale and force are clearly spiritual. These judgments are meant to shake the world, to bring it to its knees. This is destruction on a vast scale—yet not total. Even in wrath, God does not act without measure. These judgments reveal both his justice and his patience. To John's audience, these images would resonate with fear of invasion from the East—the Euphrates marked the Roman frontier. Yet the vision makes clear that these forces are spiritual, and however or whenever they play out in the natural world is under his divine command.[1]

However, the response is heartbreaking. This is the true tragedy of the trumpet judgments—not the destruction, but the refusal to repent. The human heart, hardened in rebellion, rejects even the clearest warnings. This closing note is the most tragic. After all the warnings, judgments, and signs, the survivors still refuse to repent. Their rejection of God is not based on ignorance but on willful rebellion. The human heart, hardened by sin, resists even the clearest call to turn.

Understanding the Trumpets

When reading Revelation chapters 8 and 9, the reader should not get lost in trying to pinpoint exactly when these trumpet judgments have occurred—or if they are yet to come. That kind of speculation often distracts from the message of Revelation. These events are not meant to feed curiosity but to stir the conscience. God is actively speaking through the brokenness of the world, calling nations and individuals to repent before it is too late. As believers, the focus should be on proclaiming Christ and urging people to respond to his mercy while the door is still open. As the rest of Revelation will make clear, the seventh trumpet unleashes the final outpouring of God's wrath. One thing is for certain: this has not yet happened, since the world still exists and Jesus has not yet returned. For church leaders and believers—especially those under persecution—this section is sobering but also encouraging. God's people are not forgotten in the chaos. They are sealed, marked as belonging to him. They may suffer as the world shakes,

---

1. Keener, *Revelation*, 270–74.

The Trumpets as Wake-Up Calls

but they will not be lost. The Lamb is still leading history forward. These trumpet judgments remind the church that history is not spiraling; it is being steered.

Why It Still Matters Today

Jesus warned that at his return "it will be as it was in the days of Noah" (Luke 17:26)—people eating and drinking, marrying and giving in marriage (Matt 24:37–39; Luke 17:26–30). In other words, life will be business as usual. History shows that even after disasters, wars, or pandemics shake us awake for a time, the world soon slides back into ordinary routines as if nothing eternal is at stake. We treat God's alarms as temporary interruptions rather than invitations to repent, and in doing so, we prove how fragile our sense of security really is.

The sobering truth in Rev 9 is that warning alone does not guarantee repentance. Human hearts today are just as prone to hardening in the face of truth as Pharaoh's was during the plagues of Egypt. That means every crisis—whether personal, national, or global—presents us with a choice: to turn toward God in humility or to retreat further into self-reliance and rebellion.

For the church, this section calls us to urgency in prayer, witness, and self-examination. God's window of mercy remains open, but it will not stay open forever. The challenge of these chapters is to respond while there is still time—and to urge others to do the same.

Questions for Reflection and Discussion

- What do the trumpet judgments reveal about the state of the world—and God's response to it?
- The trumpet judgments are severe, yet still partial—showing God's mercy in giving space for repentance. Where in your own life do you see God's mercy calling you to greater readiness, repentance, or faithfulness?

- Since Revelation emphasizes readiness over speculation about timelines, how can church leaders and believers guard against distraction by predictions and instead lead others to repentance and faith in Christ?

CHAPTER SIX

The Angel and the Temple of God

What John Sees

A MIGHTY ANGEL DESCENDS, wrapped in a cloud with a rainbow above his head, his face shining like the sun and his legs like pillars of fire. Seven thunders speak but are sealed. The angel swears there will be no more delay, and John is told to measure the temple.

Reference: Revelation 10—11:2

The Angel

Revelation 10 introduces a dramatic pause between the sixth and seventh trumpet judgments. This is not a delay caused by uncertainty but a deliberate interlude—a solemn pause in which heaven pulls back the curtain to give the church perspective before the next wave of judgment unfolds.

A mighty angel descends from heaven, planting one foot on the sea and the other on the land, signaling that what is about to happen will affect the whole earth—no corner of creation is outside the reach of God's sovereign plan. The presence of the rainbow is deeply significant. It echoes the covenant God made with Noah after the flood, as recorded in Genesis. The rainbow was the sign of God's promise never again to destroy humanity by water. In

Revelation, its appearance over the angel's head connects what is unfolding to that covenant faithfulness. It reassures the reader that God's justice is never divorced from his mercy, and he is always true to his promises.

The angel holds a small scroll, signifying a message from God that is about to be delivered. When he cries out, seven thunders respond with their own voices, yet John is told to seal up what they reveal. This rare moment of withheld revelation reminds us that while God reveals much, some mysteries remain hidden.

Then the angel swears an oath, echoing Dan 12:7, but with one key difference: in Daniel, there is a delay; here, the angel declares that there will be no more delay. Notably, the angel in both Daniel and Revelation stands with hands raised to heaven and declares an oath by God, showing a striking continuity between the two visions. This shared posture emphasizes the connection between Daniel's prophecy of the end times and the fulfillment now being revealed to John. God's plan is moving to its final stage. The mystery of God—his redemptive purpose—is about to be fulfilled.

John is then commanded to take the scroll from the angel's hand and eat it. This act echoes the prophetic tradition, particularly in Ezek 2–3, where the prophet is likewise told to consume a scroll containing God's message. In both cases, the eating of the scroll symbolizes the prophet's total internalization of the divine word—a taking in of God's revelation that goes beyond mere hearing. It becomes part of the prophet's very being.

The scroll is described as sweet as honey in John's mouth, yet it turns bitter in his stomach. This dual reaction captures a profound theological tension at the heart of Revelation: the message of God is both glorious and grievous. The sweetness reflects the beauty, truth, and ultimate victory of God's purposes—the hope of redemption and the establishment of Christ's kingdom. The bitterness reflects the judgment, suffering, and wrath that are also part of the prophetic message.

This moment affirms John's role not just as a visionary but as a prophetic mouthpiece. He must proclaim a message that is both life giving and devastating. Just as Ezekiel was commissioned to speak words of both warning and hope to rebellious Israel, John is now prepared to speak a word that spans salvation and judgment—a word that will confront the powers of the world and call the churches to endurance and faithfulness.

In short, the eating of the scroll is not just a ritual but a prophetic commissioning. The word must be digested, not merely delivered. And the prophet must bear both its sweetness and its sting.

The Temple of God

In the New Testament, the temple is not merely a physical structure—it is the covenant people of God, made up of both believing Jews and gentiles. As Paul teaches in 1 Cor 3 and Eph 2, the church is God's temple, indwelt by his Spirit. John carries that same motif in Revelation. When he is told to measure the temple, it signifies God's protection and ownership of his people.

At the same time, the vision seems to communicate multiple layers of meaning. The trampling of the outer court likely reflects both the historical defilement of the temple site in Jerusalem and echoes Jesus's warnings in Matt 24 and Luke 21 (see the excursus at the end of chapter 7).

Later in chapter 11 of Revelation—after the two witnesses have testified, been opposed, and vindicated—the seventh trumpet sounds, and the heavenly temple is opened. This fulfills what Hebrews teaches: the earthly temple was always a shadow of the true spiritual sanctuary in heaven. The ark of the covenant is revealed—a sign of God's presence and faithfulness—as his redemptive plan reaches its climax.

What It Still Means Today

The vision of the scroll reminds the church that God's word is both sweet and bitter—sweet because it announces forgiveness, hope, and eternal life to those who believe; bitter because it confronts the darkness of sin and warns of judgment for those who reject

God's grace. The sweetness is the joy of the gospel: the promise that Christ has conquered sin and death and offers reconciliation to all who trust in him. The bitterness comes from the reality that not everyone will receive this good news, and that God's people are often called to proclaim truths the world does not want to hear.

Like John eating the scroll, every believer is called to take in the whole counsel of God's word, not just the parts that are comforting or inspiring. We must embrace the truth in its fullness—both the promises that encourage us and the warnings that challenge us. This means proclaiming God's message with love and humility, even when it is costly, unpopular, or opposed. Faithfulness to Christ requires us to speak the truth because it is God's word, not because it will be readily received.

The measuring of the temple reassures the church that even when trials, persecution, or suffering come, God's people are not abandoned or overlooked. To be measured is to be known, counted, and set apart as belonging to him. This act signifies that the Lord knows every one of his own and places his protection around them. While the church may be harmed physically or opposed by the powers of this world, its spiritual security is unshakable in Christ.

This vision reminds us that our ultimate safety does not rest in earthly circumstances, government protection, or personal strength. Our security rests in belonging to Christ—sealed by his Spirit, preserved by his grace, and held in his hands. Even in seasons of uncertainty, we can trust that God sees us, measures us as his own, and will keep us safe for eternity.

The Word of Their Testimony

A local leader paid a high price for his faith. His wife filed for divorce because of his commitment to Christ—finalized instantly under local law. Then, he was sentenced to prison for preaching the gospel. One fellow believer didn't call it a testimony, but a spiritual alarm: a call to pray and war in the heavenlies. In hostile places, endurance isn't abstract—it's personal. And when one member suffers, the whole church is called to stand.

Questions for Reflection and Discussion

- John found the scroll sweet to the taste yet bitter in his stomach. How do you experience both the comfort and challenge of God's word in your own life?
- The angel declared there would be no more delay. How does this assurance of God's timetable encourage you to trust his plan in uncertain times?
- What does the measuring of the temple teach us about God's protection of his people, especially when they face hardship or persecution?

CHAPTER SEVEN

The Two Witnesses

What John Sees

JOHN SEES TWO WITNESSES empowered by God to proclaim the truth with boldness for a set time. Though opposed, killed, and dishonored by the world, they are raised to life and taken up to heaven. As the seventh trumpet sounds, heaven declares that the kingdom of the world now belongs to the Lord and his Christ.

Reference: Revelation chapter 11:3–19

Two Witnesses Are Revealed

Revelation chapter 11 introduces a mysterious vision of two witnesses who prophesy for 1,260 days, clothed in sackcloth. This period—also described elsewhere in Scripture as 42 months or "a time, times, and half a time" (Dan 7:25; 12:7, 11–13; Rev 11:2–3; 12:6, 14; 13:5)—is central to understanding both Daniel's visions and John's prophecy. In Revelation, the 1,260 days symbolize the entire tribulation age, stretching from Christ's ascension until his return, as the next chapter of Revelation will make clear. Because of its importance, we will examine this time frame more fully in the excursus at the end of this chapter as well.

The Two Witnesses

The witnesses are described as "the two olive trees and the two lampstands that stand before the Lord of the earth" (Rev 11:4), echoing Zech 4. In the context of Revelation, lampstands have previously symbolized churches (1:20), and olive trees are often associated with the empowering presence of the Holy Spirit (Zech 4:1-6). Also, in Scripture, two witnesses often symbolize a valid and trustworthy testimony. According to the Law, a matter was established only "on the evidence of two or three witnesses" (Deut 19:15). This principle runs throughout the Bible—Jesus sent out his disciples two by two (Mark 6:7), and even Paul said, "Every charge must be established by the evidence of two or three witnesses" (2 Cor 13:1). When we get to Rev 11, John is shown two witnesses who prophesy, confront the world's sin, and declare God's truth during a period of great opposition. These two are not random; they symbolize a faithful and divinely authorized testimony. Their presence reminds readers that God always provides a clear, sufficient witness to his truth, even in the darkest times.[1]

The witnesses are further described with powers that echo the great prophetic forerunners of Israel's story. John says they can "shut the sky so that no rain may fall" (v. 6), recalling Elijah's prayer that withheld rain in the days of Ahab (1 Kgs 17:1; Jas 5:17). He also says they can "turn water into blood and strike the earth with every kind of plague," which unmistakably recalls the signs and wonders worked through Moses in Egypt (Exod 7-12). Taken together, these parallels suggest that the two witnesses are modeled on Elijah and Moses, the archetypal prophets who confronted kings, called people to repentance, and demonstrated God's power in decisive moments of redemptive history.[2]

From this symbolic perspective, the reader can conclude that the two witnesses represent the faithful, Spirit-empowered testimony of the church amid tribulation and opposition. They embody the church's prophetic role in the world, calling people to repentance, standing against evil, enduring persecution, and preparing the way of the Lord. Their death and resurrection mirror the path

---

1. Keener, *Revelation*, 292-93.
2. Keener, *Revelation*, 289-91.

of Christ himself: suffering, apparent defeat, and ultimate vindication. The sackcloth they wear underscores a mission marked by humility, mourning, and repentance. This vision becomes a powerful picture of the church's witness in a hostile world—not only in words, but in its posture and sacrifice.

However, some evidence points to a literal fulfillment unfolding before Christ returns. The narrative includes vivid, concrete details: the witnesses' bodies lie unburied in the street; the nations celebrate their deaths; and the world watches in awe as they are raised and taken up to heaven. This level of detail supports the possibility of literal fulfillment.

The reference to Zech 4 may also lean toward a literal application. In its original context, the two olive trees represented two real individuals—Zerubbabel and Joshua—who were anointed to lead Israel's restoration. If Revelation is building on that precedent, it is reasonable to ask whether these two witnesses likewise represent two specific, anointed individuals who will arise in the last days for a prophetic mission.

The details of their resurrection after three and a half days are especially notable. A symbolic reading only sees this as a broken seven—a number often used to signify divine completeness—implying a limited, God-ordained period of suffering. But taken at face value, the exact duration, along with the public nature of their resurrection and ascension, strengthens the argument for a possible literal event still to come as well.

This suggests that Rev 11 likely operates on more than one level. The two witnesses could be literal, Spirit-anointed individuals sent by God toward the very last days. At the same time, they also reflect the ongoing prophetic role of the church—faithful, suffering, and ultimately vindicated. As with many biblical prophecies, this vision may be typological: portraying a future historical event that also embodies enduring spiritual truths. A clear example of this pattern appears in the book of Isaiah. In Isa 7:14, the prophet declares: "Behold, the virgin shall conceive and bear a son, and shall call his name Immanuel." While Christians rightly see this as a messianic prophecy fulfilled in Jesus, Isaiah's original context shows an earlier, immediate fulfillment. The child is a sign to King Ahaz, and Isaiah goes on to say that before the child knows how to refuse evil and choose good—in other words, before he is weaned—specific events will happen. However, the Gospel of Matthew later points to this same verse (Isa 7:14) as fulfilled again in the virgin birth of Jesus (Matt 1:22–23). This is a classic case of double fulfillment: the prophecy had a real, immediate meaning in Isaiah's day and a deeper, ultimate fulfillment in the birth of Christ.

Therefore, the timing and imagery here in Rev 11 may serve a dual purpose—strengthen the church's present calling to bear witness in the face of opposition, while also pointing forward to a specific prophetic event still to come. Just as Jesus fulfilled prophecy both literally and symbolically, the two witnesses may stand at the intersection of symbolism and historical reality.

This balanced approach preserves theological integrity and honors the complexity of apocalyptic prophecy. It allows the church to see itself in the vision—called to witness, endure, and trust God—while remaining open to a future moment where two literal witnesses will dramatically testify to the truth in the final days.

The Seventh Trumpet

After the resurrection and ascension of the two witnesses, the seventh trumpet sounds—a moment of climax in the narrative. Loud voices in heaven proclaim that "the kingdom of the world has become the kingdom of our Lord and of his Christ" (v. 15), signaling the full establishment of Christ's reign. This moment marks the culmination of the church's witness, the resurrection of the saints, and the beginning of final judgment on the wicked.

The twenty-four elders fall in worship, giving thanks that God's plan has reached its appointed end. The time has come to reward his servants and to bring justice upon the earth. Thunder, lightning, earthquakes, and hail follow—cosmic signs that the final outpouring of divine wrath is about to begin.

This seventh trumpet appears to correspond with the "last trumpet" Paul describes in 1 Thess 4:16 and 1 Cor 15:52—when the dead in Christ are raised and the living are caught up to meet the Lord. Just as the seventh trumpet signals the final stage of redemptive history in Revelation, Paul's writings connect the last trumpet blast with resurrection and transformation.

It's also significant that John hears the sounding of the seventh trumpet after seeing the two witnesses taken up to heaven. Their bodily resurrection mirrors the "first resurrection" John will describe later (Rev 20:5–6). This connection suggests that their ascension is not merely a dramatic escape, but a foreshadowing of the larger resurrection and vindication of all God's people. They are not rescued from general tribulation, but from the final outpouring of wrath that is about to fall on the unrepentant world.

In this light, the seventh trumpet stands as a turning point—closing the church's age of prophetic witness and opening the final movement of judgment and victory. The faithful testimony of God's people is complete. Now, the King reigns.

Why It Still Matters Today

Revelation 10–11 gives the church its marching orders in the middle of tribulation: speak the word and stand as witnesses—no matter the cost. Whether the two witnesses are symbolic of the church or literal end-time prophets (or both), the message remains the same: God's people are called to proclaim truth, endure suffering, and trust in the certainty of Christ's victory.

The seventh trumpet doesn't sound with fear, but with finality. It announces what the church has long hoped for: Christ reigns. "The kingdom of the world has become the kingdom of our Lord and of his Christ, and he shall reign forever and ever."

The Two Witnesses

Questions for Reflection and Discussion

- In what ways does your church—or you personally—reflect the calling to be a faithful witness during times of pressure or hardship?
- What encouragement can we draw from the promise that suffering has an end and that Jesus will reign?
- Why is it important to hold both symbolic and literal layers of prophecy in tension rather than choosing one exclusively?

Excursus

The 1,260 Days—From Daniel to Revelation

THE "1,260 DAYS"—ALSO EXPRESSED as 42 months or "a time, times, and half a time"—emerge first in Daniel's visions and reappear throughout Revelation. To understand their meaning in John's prophecy, we must trace how the Bible develops this time frame. In Daniel, the number refers to a literal period of days. Historically, this period is connected to the severe persecution under Antiochus Epiphanes in the second century BC. During his reign, the Jewish temple was defiled. He sacrificed a pig to Zeus on the altar and stopped Jewish worship for three and a half years, marking a clear desecration of the sanctuary.

Daniel's visions (Dan 9:25–26) connected the desecration of the temple with the coming of the Anointed One and the end. This is why many in Jesus's day expected the Messiah to appear soon after such events. Thus, when Jesus predicted the destruction of the temple (Matt 24:2), his disciples asked: "When will this happen, and what will be the sign of your coming and of the end of the age?" (v. 3). They linked both the temple's desecration and destruction with both of the Messiah's comings because Daniel had placed them side by side.

Jesus confirmed that Daniel's prophecy would be fulfilled in the destruction of Jerusalem. In Matt 24:15 and Mark 13:14, he

Excursus

explicitly referred to "the abomination of desolation spoken of by the prophet Daniel." When the Romans destroyed the temple in AD 70, Daniel's vision advanced: the sanctuary was ruined, the sacrifices ceased, and the abomination reached a new peak. That's why Matthew urged his readers to pay close attention because they believed Daniel's prophecy had already been fulfilled during the Maccabean Revolt. But Jesus reinterpreted it. Luke, writing for a non-Jewish audience, translated and clarified Jesus's warning: "When you see Jerusalem surrounded by armies, then know that its desolation has come near" (Luke 21:20). And he added, "Jerusalem will be trampled underfoot by the gentiles, until the times of the gentiles are fulfilled" (v. 24). In other words, Jesus didn't point to a one-time event, but to an extended period of spiritual decline and foreign domination—one that would continue until his return. This period hasn't ended. Today, the Temple Mount is still under the control of a religious system that denies Christ's divinity. This visible reality reflects the ongoing spiritual desolation Jesus described. The timeline is layered: it began with the desecration by Antiochus, intensified with Rome's destruction of the temple, and has continued under centuries of gentile control. Daniel prophesied the end of sacrifice and worship in the temple—and that condition still stands. It continues as long as the place once set apart for God is occupied by those who reject him. Jesus's words linked past, present, and future. He warned his first followers about what was coming soon and prepared later generations for what was still ahead.

John takes up this prophetic framework and portrays the entire age of tribulation as lasting 1,260 days. This number is not a literal countdown but a symbolic measure of the time when the church suffers opposition and bears witness to the world. Revelation organizes this age through a sequence of judgments (see diagram). Thus, the number assures God's people that their suffering is real but limited, painful but purposeful. The 1,260 days remind us that history itself is measured by God's hand—and when the time is fulfilled, Christ will return, the trampling will end, and his kingdom will be revealed in glory.

Hope That Endures

The Sequence of Revelation

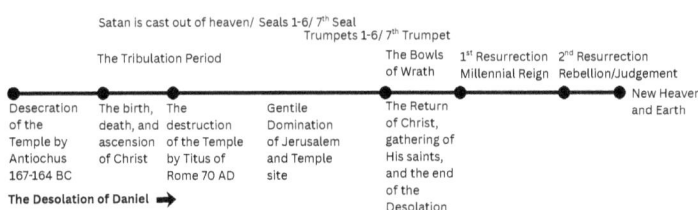

The Sequence of Revelation

CHAPTER EIGHT

The Overall Biblical Story

What John Sees

A SWEEPING VISION SHOWS a woman, a dragon, and a child. The dragon is cast down and rages against the faithful, yet the woman's offspring overcomes by the blood of the Lamb and the word of their testimony.
Reference: Revelation chapter 12

A Vision That Frames the Whole Story

Revelation 10 and 11 revealed the church's mission in the world: to prophesy, suffer, and remain faithful under pressure. The two witnesses stood as symbols of a church caught between judgment and mercy, between tribulation and ultimate glory. And when the seventh trumpet sounds, the message is unmistakable: the kingdom of Christ has come, and his reign is sure. However, Revelation isn't structured like a Western novel, which builds to a final climax. In Middle Eastern storytelling—and in much of Scripture—the climax often sits in the center, with the rest of the story radiating outward from that turning point. Revelation 12 is the center.

John's visions unfold in cycles, mirror each other, and bring the reader closer to the climax

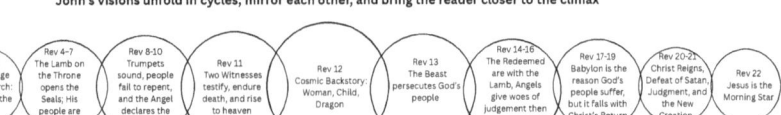

Revelation's Cycle of Visions

Revelation 12 reframes the entire book. It pulls back the curtain on the invisible war behind every visible struggle and centers the church's suffering within a cosmic drama that began with the fall of Satan and ends in Christ's return. If chapters 1–11 show the church's call to witness, chapters 12–22 reveal why the conflict is so intense—and how the victory is already secure. This central vision tells the story from heaven's perspective. It traces the spiritual battle from Genesis to the end of the age. It's not a sidebar. It's the lens through which the rest of Revelation should be read.

John sees a sweeping vision that captures the full arc of redemptive history. The woman clothed with the sun, with the moon under her feet and a crown of twelve stars, echoes Joseph's dream in Gen 37. In that dream, the sun, moon, and stars symbolized his family—Jacob, Rachel, and the twelve tribes of Israel. This confirms that the woman represents God's covenant people. Her child is Christ, born to fulfill the promises made to Abraham and David. After his resurrection and ascension, the dragon—Satan—redirects his rage against the woman's other offspring: Christians. These are those "who keep the commandments of God and hold to the testimony of Jesus" (Rev 12:17).

Central to this chapter is Michael the archangel, who rises to lead a heavenly war following Christ's ascension and defeat of Satan. This scene echoes Dan 12, where Michael stands in defense of God's people during a time of great distress and continues till the resurrection of the righteous. The war in heaven that Michael leads is not just a heavenly skirmish—it signals that the decisive turning point of history has already been reached in Christ's death, resurrection, and ascension. Michael's rising confirms that the

The Overall Biblical Story

afflictions first endured by God's people initiated by Antiochus Epiphanes that were prophesied in Dan 10-11, foreshadow the greater tribulation the church must endure before the resurrection. What Daniel saw in shadows is fulfilled in Christ and his church. In both books, Michael's intervention marks a decisive shift in the cosmic conflict—one that reverberates in both heaven and on earth. Michael's triumph results in Satan's expulsion from heaven, marking the beginning of the final phase of redemptive history. The accuser is expelled from the heavenly court, no longer able to bring charges against the saints (Rev 12:10).

Yet the narrative does not end in triumph alone. Satan, filled with fury at his defeat, intensifies his assault on the woman. However, God carries her into the wilderness. This image draws directly from Israel's story in the exodus, where the wilderness was both a place of trial and of God's faithful provision. The wilderness is not abandonment; it is preservation. It is where God's people are stripped of self-reliance and taught to depend on him alone.

The woman is nourished and preserved by God for "a time, times, and half a time," which is another reference to the prophetic period recorded in Dan 12. As explored in the excursus after chapter 7, this phrase reflects a symbolic pattern grounded in historical reality—beginning with the Maccabean persecution, echoed in the destruction of the temple in AD 70, and extending through the church's witness and suffering until Christ's return. John frames it as the defined, limited season of suffering and witness for those who believe and follow Christ between his ascension and return. It is not an endless struggle but a bounded one. Satan knows his time is short, and so he rages with fury, yet his defeat is certain.

If Satan becomes more aggressive after being cast down, then the text presents a sequence: his fall unleashes a period of growing persecution. Revelation 12 should therefore be read as depicting both inaugurated and escalating realities. The initial victory—Christ's ascension and Satan's expulsion—is historical and decisive. But the dragon's vengeance, particularly his war against the woman's offspring, is an ongoing drama throughout the tribulation age and will intensify as the end draws near. Persecution is not simply a relic of the past; it is the church's present and expected future.

Theologically, this reinforces the already-but-not-yet tension. Christ reigns. Satan's authority is broken. But the final conflict is still playing out. Christians live in the crosshairs of that conflict. The dragon, cast down and enraged, pursues God's people with ferocity. But his time is short. His defeat is certain.

However, the path of victory is not through force but through faithfulness. Christians prevail not with swords or systems but by clinging to Christ's sacrifice and boldly bearing witness, even in the face of death. Revelation 12:11 gives us the blueprint: "They overcame him by the blood of the Lamb and by the word of their testimony, for they did not love their lives even unto death." Leaders must continually return to this truth. Victory is already secured through Jesus. The testimony of believers—their public allegiance to Christ—is a weapon against fear and compromise. When the church chooses faithfulness over safety, the enemy loses again and again.

This vision offers no promise of comfort—but it does offer clarity. Suffering is not meaningless. It is the expected cost of following Christ in a hostile world. The faithful church, especially in the 10/40 Window (see glossary), is not forgotten. The wilderness is not abandonment. It is where God matures and preserves his people. Leaders must hold this perspective—and pass it on. When fear rises, they point to God's faithfulness. When pressure builds, they call for endurance.

Why It Still Matters Today

Revelation 12 is the heart of John's Apocalypse, reminding us that endurance is victory through the blood of the Lamb and the word of our testimony. This vision John sees gives us our identity and strategy as believers. We are the woman's offspring—protected in the wilderness, nourished by God, marked by our testimony to Christ. We stand in continuity with Daniel's vision: tribulation comes, Michael rises, names recorded in the book of life are

The Overall Biblical Story

preserved, resurrection follows, and final victory belongs to the Lord. The wilderness is not the end of the story; it is the place where God keeps his people until the story's end arrives. For those walking with the persecuted church, this vision is more than explanation—it is strength. It reminds us that our suffering fits into the larger pattern of redemption, and that the Lamb who was slain now reigns and ensures his people will overcome.

The Word of Their Testimony

As a boy, he had a vivid dream about the end of the world. He saw the earth begin to collapse and sink, and just as it vanished beneath him, someone appeared, grabbed his hand, and lifted him to safety. He had no idea the imagery came straight from the book of Revelation. Raised in a different faith, he spent years shaped by those teachings. But over time, he began to compare what he'd learned to what he read in the Bible. One by one, the claims of Scripture stood out with clarity and power. Eventually, he surrendered his life to Jesus—and was baptized. The hand that lifted him in the dream is the same hand that now holds his life.

Questions for Reflection and Discussion

- How does Rev 12 help clarify the spiritual nature of persecution, specifically in the 10/40 Window today?
- What does the wilderness represent in a believer's life, and how is it also a place of preservation?
- What are practical ways to help believers grow in the word of their testimony?
- How does the promise of a limited tribulation period change the way leaders view long-term suffering?
- Why is it important to lead not with promises of ease but with a vision of eternal victory?

CHAPTER NINE

Beasts Rise

What John Sees

TWO BEASTS ARISE—ONE WIELDING political power, the other spreading deception—pressing the world into idolatry and marking its followers for wrath and destruction. Yet the Lamb stands on Mount Zion with his redeemed, sealed with his name, destined for victory.

Reference: Revelation chapters 13—14:5

Beasts from the Sea and Earth

If chapter 12 is the theological center of the book, chapter 13 shows its unfolding consequences. The dragon, cast down and enraged, now empowers earthly systems to wage war on God's people. What follows is not a new story, but a deeper layer of the same one—a revealing of how the spiritual war plays out on the ground: through politics, propaganda, idolatry, persecution, and, ultimately, judgment.

John sees two beasts that rise to challenge God and wage war against his people. The first beast comes from the sea, a symbol

Beasts Rise

throughout Scripture of chaos and spiritual darkness.[1] This also draws from Dan 7, where beasts represent empires that rise from turbulent nations to dominate the earth. Like those empires, the sea beast blasphemes God, wages war against the saints, and receives its authority from the dragon—portraying a political system or ruler empowered by Satan to oppose God's people. John describes this beast as having ten horns and ten diadems (Rev 13:1), language that draws directly from Dan 7:7, 24, where horns symbolize kings or kingdoms that arise from the empires of the world. In Scripture, horns consistently represent ruling power or authority (see also Dan 8:20–21; Rev 17:12). The number ten is not merely pointing to ten literal kings/emperors. It conveys completeness in earthly power and human responsibility before God—as seen earlier in Rev 2:10 regarding the church in Smyrna's ten days of testing. Thus, the beast's seven heads with ten crowned horns portray the full measure of political authority that earthly rulers and empires wield in opposition to God's kingdom—power that is real but limited and temporary under God's sovereignty.

The second beast, from the earth, stands for deceptive religious influence that supports and legitimizes the power of the first. It performs signs, compels worship, and creates an image of the first beast to be honored. Rather than pointing people to the truth, it misleads them into allegiance with evil. This beast shows how religious systems can be twisted to serve corrupt powers instead of God's kingdom.

In this same passage, John also refers to the number 666, which seems to be a coded reference to Nero Caesar. Using gematria—an ancient system in which letters were assigned numerical values—the name "Nero Caesar" in Hebrew adds up to 666.[2] This was not a random number. It symbolized a ruler who embodied evil, demanded divine worship, and brought brutal persecution on the church. The number would have been immediately understood by John's original audience as a sign of a tyrannical, godless ruler (1 John 2:18–19; 4:3).

---

1. Walton, *Genesis*, 67–76.
2. Keener, *Revelation*, 354–56.

These beasts clearly pointed to the Roman Empire. Emperors like Nero and Domitian—the emperor during the time John received and recorded the Revelation—violently persecuted the church and demanded worship as divine.

However, the vision is not limited to the first century. These beasts represent that same recurring pattern of power that appears throughout history: governments that demand ultimate allegiance, systems that distort truth, and rulers who exalt themselves in the place of God.

Ultimately, there will likely be a final ruler—a last embodiment of the beast—who will rise in opposition to Christ and lead a global rebellion. He will gather everything that has stood against God into one final surge of defiance. Like the powers before him, his end is certain: he will be judged at Christ's return (2 Thess 2:3–8).

This second beast also reflects the kind of religious deception Paul attributes to the "man of lawlessness" and what John describes as the spirit of the "antichrist." For a fuller discussion of how these figures relate to Revelation's beasts, see the excursus at the end of this chapter.

This vision prepares the church to recognize the true nature of political and spiritual opposition. What may appear like ordinary governance or cultural movements can, in fact, be expressions of spiritual rebellion. The church must see clearly: behind earthly powers, there is a spiritual enemy who wages war—but whose time is short.

The Redeemed with the Lamb

The vision now shifts from the terror of the beast to the triumph of the Lamb. In contrast with those bearing the mark of the beast, John, once again, hears the number 144,000 and sees the multitudes of the redeemed, which are one and the same. They are standing with the Lamb on Mount Zion. This is more than a glimpse of the future; it is a deliberate theological statement placed here before the bowls of wrath are unleashed. Revelation anchors the reader in this truth: the redeemed are with Christ. They will not face the wrath of God falling on the earth. This is the answer to the question raised earlier—"Who can stand?" (6:17). The church can stand, not by its own strength, but because it is sealed and preserved by the Lamb. What follows in the pouring out of the bowls is not judgment on God's people but judgment on rebellion. Scripture consistently distinguishes between tribulation, which the church endures, and wrath, which is reserved for the ungodly. Christians may suffer under the rage of the beast, but they are never the objects of God's wrath. That wrath is poured out on those who bear the mark of the beast, while those sealed with the Lamb's name stand safe in his presence.

This vision is pastoral reassurance for the church. Before the bowls are described in their terrible completeness, John shows the redeemed already with Christ, singing a new song. Their song is unique—one that only the redeemed can learn. It is the song of endurance, faithfulness, and victory through suffering. Their voices stand in stark contrast to the roar of those who follow the beast. Where the world resounds with fear, rebellion, and idolatry, the people of God respond with worship, loyalty, and triumph in the Lamb.

The placement of this vision is crucial. God never reveals judgment without also showing his people secure in his presence. Just as Rev 7 showed the sealing of the saints before the trumpets, so here Rev 14 shows the redeemed with the Lamb before the bowls. The message is unmistakable: when God pours out his wrath on the rebellious, his people are with him. This does not mean the church is spared from suffering, but it does mean the church is saved from the wrath of God that is coming. The redeemed stand with the Lamb, and nothing—not beast, not bowls of wrath—can separate them from his care.

John also describes these redeemed ones as those "who have not defiled themselves with women, for they are virgins" (v. 4). This language is not meant to suggest literal celibacy or to disparage marriage, which Scripture honors as holy (Heb 13:4). Rather, it draws on the prophetic imagery of the Old Testament, where idolatry was often portrayed as spiritual adultery against God (Hos 1–4; Jer 3:6–10; Ezek 16:23). To be "undefiled" and called "virgins" is to be wholly devoted to Christ, refusing the spiritual fornication of Babylon and the worship of the beast. Like Paul's image of presenting the church as a pure virgin to Christ (2 Cor 11:2), it highlights undivided loyalty to the Lamb.

The emphasis, then, is not on their marital status but on their loyalty: they have resisted the world's seduction and remained faithful to the Lamb. This description is meant to encourage every believer living under pressure: God sees those who refuse compromise, who keep themselves spiritually pure amid a corrupt world. Their faithfulness assures them that they belong to the Lamb and will share in his victory.

Why It Still Matters Today

These chapters speak powerfully to Christians living under pressure. The vision of the 144,000 reminds us that what defines the redeemed is not political power or earthly security but faithful allegiance to Christ in a hostile world. Revelation does not hide the reality of suffering; it explains it. The beasts rise and thrive, but only for a time. The church is not left to wonder whether God sees or cares; he sees every injustice, hears every cry, and will respond. The message is not simply that the church wins—it is that Christ reigns. The Lamb is not only Savior—he is Judge. The systems of this world may seem unshakable, but every government that opposes God will fall. The church's hope is not in escaping tribulation but in standing firm through it, knowing that justice is coming and that Christ will be revealed in glory.

THE WORD OF THEIR TESTIMONY

A sister in Christ, once hesitant and quiet, has become fearless in sharing her faith. Despite personal challenges and societal pressure, she said she can no longer stay silent about Jesus—no matter the cost. Her passion is unshaken, and her witness has begun to impact those around her. In an environment that often demands silence, her boldness reflects the Spirit's power to transform fear into courage.

Questions for Reflection and Discussion

- How can Christian leaders help the church discern the presence of beast-like powers in today's world?
- In what ways does Revelation equip the church to interpret opposition through a spiritual lens?
- Revelation 14:4 describes the redeemed as those who have remained faithful and undefiled amidst a corrupt world. In what ways are Christians today tempted to compromise their allegiance to Christ, and what practices help us stay loyal to the Lamb when the pressure to conform is strong?

Excursus

Who Is the Antichrist?
A Biblical Pattern and a Personal Future

THE FIGURE OFTEN CALLED the antichrist is not confined to a single future event. The New Testament gives us a broader, layered understanding. John writes that "many antichrists have come" (1 John 2:18), describing an ongoing spirit of deception that opposes Christ and denies the truth. Paul refers to a "man of lawlessness" who will be revealed before Christ returns—someone who exalts himself, performs false signs, and leads many astray (2 Thess 2:3–8). Yet Paul also says, "The mystery of lawlessness is already at work" (v. 7), meaning this is not just a future crisis, but an active force in the present.

Taken together, these passages show that the antichrist is both:

- A spiritual pattern: an ongoing rebellion seen in rulers, systems, and ideologies that distort truth and oppose God.

- A personal future figure: someone who will ultimately embody that rebellion in a climactic way before Christ returns.

Revelation reflects both dimensions. In chapter 13, the beast from the sea and the beast from the earth show how Satan's influence works through political oppression and religious deception.

Excursus

These beasts aren't just future threats—they represent powers already active in John's time and in every generation. But Revelation also points forward to a final global rebellion, where these patterns will intensify and culminate in open opposition to Christ and his people.

The antichrist, then, is not just a name for one end-times villain. It's a biblical warning about both the systems of evil we must resist now and the ultimate showdown we await with hope in the returning King.

CHAPTER TEN

The Bowls of Wrath

What John Sees

THE LAMB BEGINS HIS harvest—having gathered his redeemed, he now treads the winepress of God's wrath. Seven angels pour out the bowls, unleashing the final plagues on the beast's kingdom. God's holiness and justice are fully displayed as his wrath reaches its completion.

Reference: Revelation chapters 14:6—16:21

The Bowls of Wrath

Immediately after showing the redeemed with the Lamb, John turns to visions of judgment. Three angels appear, each delivering a universal message to the world. The first proclaims the eternal gospel to every nation, tribe, language, and people. Even in the last days, God's mercy continues to be offered, and his mission to call the nations to repentance remains unchanged. The second angel announces the fall of Babylon. In John's time, Babylon pointed to Rome—the dominant power hostile to God and oppressive toward his people. But Babylon is more than a historical reference. It is a recurring symbol of human systems in rebellion against God. Whether it is Rome, a modern empire, or a future global power,

The Bowls of Wrath

every Babylon will fall. The final Babylon—still to come—will embody this defiance in its fullest form, and its collapse will signal the end of human pride and resistance to God's rule.

The third angel delivers a sobering warning: those who worship the beast and receive its mark will face God's wrath. The language is vivid and final—torment, fire, sulfur, and unending judgment. There will be no rest for those aligned with the beast. In contrast, a voice from heaven affirms that those who "die in the Lord from now on" (14:13) are blessed—indicating that this promise applies beginning in John's present moment.

Though Christians may suffer, they will one day rest, and their faithful deeds will follow them. This leads to a powerful call for endurance. God's people are urged to remain steadfast, keeping his commandments and holding fast to their faith in Jesus. The vision closes with two harvest scenes, drawn from Old Testament imagery. The first is a harvest of righteousness, where the Son of Man reaps the earth. The second is a harvest of judgment, where an angel gathers grapes and casts them into the winepress of God's wrath. Blood flows as high as a horse's bridle for "1,600 stadia" (184 miles), an image of total and terrifying judgment.

This vision introduces the coming judgment in symbolic form. The same realities will soon be revisited and expanded in the bowl judgments. But even here the message is clear: Christ will return, justice will be done, and the redeemed must endure until the end.

John then sees the final stage of judgment initiated. Seven angels appear with seven bowls filled with the wrath of God. These bowls are poured out after the opening of the heavenly tabernacle, reminding the reader of when the seventh trumpet was blown. This moment signals the conclusion of God's patient warnings and the beginning of final justice. Each bowl targets a specific area of creation or society. The first brings painful sores upon idolaters. The second and third turn seas and rivers to blood. The fourth scorches the earth with fire. The fifth strikes the throne of the beast, while the sixth prepares the way for the final battle. The seventh brings total collapse. These judgments echo the plagues of Egypt, but on a global scale, showing that just as God judged Pharaoh for oppressing his people, he will once again judge all who refuse to repent and who persecute the righteous.

These acts of judgment are not uncontrolled outbursts of divine anger. They are holy, measured, and justified. God has offered grace. The gospel has gone out. The nations have had their opportunity. But where there is no repentance, judgment must follow. For the persecuted church, this is both a warning and comfort. God sees, remembers, and now he acts. Those who suffer now will one day see the fall of their oppressors. The bowls remind the church that while wrath is terrifying, it is also righteous. God is not slow to judge—he is patient in mercy. But in the end, his justice will be seen.

To John's audience, each bowl carried vivid meaning. The first bowl, bringing painful sores, recalled the plagues of Egypt, reminding believers that allegiance has consequences. The second and third bowls, turning waters to blood, echoed Exod 7. For persecuted believers, this judgment was personal: "They have shed our blood; now they drink it" (Rev 16:6). The fourth bowl scorched the earth with heat, yet rather than repent, people cursed God, demonstrating the hardness of the human heart. The fifth plunged the beast's throne into darkness, showing that no empire was beyond God's reach. The sixth prepared for Armageddon—a symbolic vision of the final confrontation between good and evil—reminding believers to remain spiritually alert, for the nations will one day march out against the returning Christ, and his judgment will fall. Finally, the seventh bowl completes the series: "It is done" (v. 17). The earth shakes, cities collapse, and Babylon—the symbol of worldly rebellion—is destroyed. For John's readers, this meant Rome's glory would not endure. For today's church, it means no worldly power will ultimately stand. Christ will reign.

Together, these bowls paint a picture of final judgment. They are not random, vengeful acts but righteous and purposeful justice. They vindicate the suffering church and confront an unrepentant world. The call remains the same as it has throughout Revelation: endure, be faithful, and stay awake.

The Bowls of Wrath

A key difference between the trumpet judgments (Rev 8–11) and the bowl judgments (Rev 16) is scope and intent. The trumpet judgments affected a third of the earth—vegetation, waters, and people—indicating restraint and extending an invitation to repentance. The bowls, however, are total. No longer is there a fraction withheld; judgment falls on the entire earth. With the trumpets, repentance was still possible. But Rev 9 records that even after terrifying plagues, "they did not repent" (vv. 20–21). With the bowls, the time for mercy has passed. These are not warnings but conclusions. This is the execution of divine justice in full measure.

This global scope and irreversible nature of the bowls align with Old Testament prophecy about "the great and terrible day of the Lord." The prophets spoke of that day as the time when God would judge the nations, shake the heavens and the earth, and pour out wrath against all wickedness (see Joel 2:1–11; Isa 13; Zeph 1). The bowls represent that final day, when no injustice is overlooked and no rebellion ignored.

Why It Still Matters Today

Just as earlier chapters presented a series of visions—seals, trumpets, and witnesses—chapters 13 to 16 continue with beasts, warnings, and bowls. These are not strictly linear events, as if each chapter were a date on a calendar. Revelation doesn't move like a timeline—it moves like a spiral: circling the same themes with growing intensity, each cycle bringing us closer to the final confrontation. There is a sequence—but not a rigid one. The visions escalate. The opposition becomes clearer. The judgment becomes fuller, and hope becomes brighter. The seals, trumpets, and bowls are not disconnected or redundant but layered. Evil grows bolder. Judgment grows fuller. Christ's reign draws nearer. The end is not repetitive—it is rising.

This vision of rising conflict and judgment calls us to live with clear eyes and steadfast hearts. We shouldn't be surprised when evil seems to escalate in the world around us; Revelation shows us that as the return of Christ draws near, the opposition to his kingdom grows louder and more defiant. Instead of panicking or retreating, we are invited to stand firm in the confidence that Jesus remains on the throne and none of this takes him by surprise. The judgments remind us that God is neither indifferent nor slow to act—he warns and calls the world to repentance before the final day. For those in Christ, these judgments deepen our gratitude, for he has borne the wrath we deserved; for those who don't yet know him, they stir us to urgency in sharing the gospel. And as the spiral tightens and the darkness deepens, hope shines even brighter: the Lamb is coming, his victory is sure, and his reign is drawing near. That hope is not meant to be distant or abstract—it anchors us to live faithfully today, with holiness in our hearts, courage in our witness, and watchfulness in our daily walk. Revelation's spiral of visions isn't meant to leave us fearful or confused but to keep us awake, ready, and eager for the day the Lamb will make all things new.

The Word of Their Testimony

After losing his job because of his faith, one believer was resourced to serve through an online ministry. He now speaks daily with people—many from a non-Christian background—who are curious about Jesus. Almost 100 percent of those he speaks with want to understand the Christian faith. What began as a setback became a front-line assignment in the harvest.

Questions for Reflection and Discussion

- What does the imagery of the bowls of wrath reveal about God's character and the seriousness of sin?
- How can leaders prepare the church for endurance—not escape—during increasing tribulation?
- Explain the similarities and differences between the trumpets and bowls.

CHAPTER ELEVEN

Babylon Revealed

What John Sees

BABYLON—THE SEDUCTIVE, GLOBAL SYSTEM opposed to God—is exposed and judged. Kings and merchants lament her collapse while heaven calls God's people to come out from her.
Reference: Revelation chapters 17—19:5

The Reason for the Bowls

Revelation 16 ends with the seventh bowl poured out—God's final judgment, shaking the earth and collapsing empires. But what, exactly, is being judged? Revelation 17-18 answers that question by unveiling the spiritual power behind it all: Babylon the great. This is not a new event but a deeper unveiling. The beast, the false prophet, and the bowls of wrath have been revealed. Now we are shown the root of it all—the spiritual system of idolatry and seduction that fuels rebellion against God. Babylon is not a footnote in the story. She is the center of the world's defiance, the power that corrupts kings and cultures, and her fall explains the wrath that has just been poured out.

John sees one of the most unsettling images in all of Scripture: a woman described as a prostitute, seated on a scarlet beast covered in blasphemous names. She is arrayed in purple and scarlet, adorned with jewels, and holding a golden cup filled with abominations. Written across her forehead are the words: "Babylon the great, mother of prostitutes and of the earth's abominations" (17:5). This is not the portrait of a literal woman but a symbolic picture of a global counterfeit kingdom—seductive, wealthy, and spiritually corrupt. From the Tower of Babel to the Babylonian exile, the name Babylon has always stood for human pride, idolatry, and the persecution of God's people. In Revelation, Babylon is not locked in the past. She is a spiritual force that transcends empires, operating through politics, economies, ideologies, and cultures. She entices humanity to exchange truth for lies, holiness for compromise, and allegiance to God for allegiance to self.

The scarlet beast that carries her—covered in heads and horns—echoes the imagery of Daniel and earlier chapters of Revelation. The heads represent empire, power, and anti-God authority, and the horns represent their rulers (Dan 7:8, 24–25). Babylon does not rule alone. She rides on the backs of political systems and institutions, using them to magnify her influence. Yet the partnership is short-lived. Evil always devours itself. The very powers that sustain Babylon will turn against her and bring her down. Even this, however, is not chaos. It is God's judgment, turning the rebellion of the nations back on their own heads.

For John's readers, this imagery would have been instantly recognizable. The apostle Peter himself, writing from Rome, referred to it symbolically as "Babylon" (1 Pet 5:13). And behind this language lies the prophetic vision of Dan 2. There, Nebuchadnezzar sees a statue of gold, silver, bronze, iron, and clay—each layer representing a succession of world empires. The head of gold is Babylon, but it is only the beginning. Each kingdom that follows—though different in strength and style—is still part of the same statue, the same man-made system built on pride and power. The vision climaxes when a stone "not cut by human hands" crashes against the statue, shattering it completely. That stone grows into a mountain that fills the whole earth, a picture of God's eternal kingdom (Dan 2:44-45). The message is unmistakable: every earthly empire will fall, and only Christ's kingdom will remain.

Revelation takes up that same prophetic pattern. For the first-century church, Babylon was Rome. But for the last days, Babylon represents the final, global expression of that same rebellious spirit—political, economic, cultural, and spiritual systems united in defiance of God. When John describes Babylon seated on seven hills and riding the beast, his audience would not only have thought of Rome's literal geography (Rome was built on seven hills) but of every empire that had ever lifted itself against God. And just like Daniel's statue, Babylon will fall—not by human reform or politics, but by the return of Christ, the stone that smashes every counterfeit kingdom.

The warning, however, is not only about the future. Babylon is here now. She is every system that seduces the church to blend in, to compromise, and to love the world more than Christ. She does not always persecute with violence; more often, she seduces with comfort, power, and wealth. Her collapse in Rev 18 is sudden and catastrophic. Kings, merchants, and shipmasters weep—not because of her wickedness, but because of their lost profit and luxury. Her destruction unmasks the world's addiction to her influence.

In the midst of this vision comes a voice from heaven: "Come out of her, my people, lest you take part in her sins, lest you share in her plagues" (v. 4). This command reveals two sobering truths. First, Babylon still has influence over believers. She is not distant; she touches the church, and her call to compromise must be resisted. Second, her fall is both future and present. Empires have collapsed before—Rome fell, and others after it. Each was an echo of Babylon's final end. Yet she rises again in new forms, whispering through modern ideologies, economies, and systems. To come out of her is not simply to withdraw physically but to resist spiritually—to reject her values, her idols, and her allure.

Hope That Endures

The Redeemed Rejoice

Then John hears thunderous worship in heaven: "Then I heard what seemed to be the voice of a great multitude" (19:1). This is the song of the redeemed celebrating God's justice and the fall of Babylon. Their voices proclaim that the Lord reigns and that his judgments are true and righteous.

This celebration takes place after the seventh trumpet has been blown (Rev 9), John sees the sealed and redeemed in heaven (Rev 14), and the bowls of wrath have been poured out on Babylon (Rev 15–18). The "great and terrible day of the Lord" (Joel 2:31) has passed. All evil empires have fallen and are no more.

Why It Still Matters Today

These visions are not flashbacks but the interpretation of what happens when the seventh trumpet is blown. This is how the book unfolds: visions layer upon each other, advancing the story not always in straight lines but in deepening cycles. Babylon is judged under the bowls. She is then exposed and unmasked so that God's people understand why judgment fell.

Babylon is both symbol and system, ancient and present. She is seductive and powerful, but her fall is certain. Revelation calls the church to clarity and separation, to resist her enticement and live for the Lamb. The warning is clear: Babylon will fall. The promise is greater still: Christ will reign forever.

Questions for Reflection and Discussion

- Peter and John both identified Babylon as Rome. What modern parallels do you see in political, religious, or cultural systems today?
- How does the church face the temptation of seduction more than physical persecution?

- What does it practically mean for the church to come out of Babylon?
- How can church leaders help believers recognize and resist Babylon's influence in areas like entertainment, economy, politics, and public life?

CHAPTER TWELVE

The Return and Reign of Christ

What John Sees

Hallelujahs resound in heaven as the marriage supper of the Lamb is celebrated. Christ appears as the Faithful and True Rider, returning in glory to judge and to reign. He defeats the beast and the false prophet, has Satan bound, and then rules with those who share in the first resurrection.

Reference: Revelation chapters 19:6—20:6

The Marriage Supper and Return of the Lamb

The scene then shifts, and John hears a multitude in heaven rejoicing at the marriage supper of the Lamb. This is no coincidence. The sound of praise connects directly with what has just taken place: Babylon's counterfeit banquet has collapsed in ruin, and immediately heaven bursts forth with joy at the true and enduring feast of Christ and his Bride. The contrast is intentional and profound—the clamor of corruption is silenced, giving way to the songs of covenant joy. At this marriage supper, the saints—raised in the first resurrection (Rev 20:4–6)—are clothed in fine linen, bright and clean. These garments symbolize the righteous deeds of the saints, not as the basis of their salvation but as the evidence of their faith. Thus, when John hears the multitude, he hears not only the joy of heaven but also the vindication of God's people, adorned in righteousness and welcomed into eternal communion with their Lord. Babylon's feast was fleeting and deceptive; the Lamb's feast is eternal and true.

Then John sees heaven opened and Christ returning in glory. As stated earlier, what he hears and what he sees are not random but theologically connected. He hears the worship of the redeemed, and he sees the Judge coming. Christ comes not secretly but openly, visibly, and decisively. He rides a white horse, symbolizing justice and victory, and is called Faithful and True. There is no coincidence that the rejoicing of the saints is immediately followed by the appearing of the Savior: the salvation of his people and the judgment of earth are two sides of the same climactic moment. His robe is dipped in blood, his head crowned with many diadems, and from his mouth comes a sharp sword—the power of his word—that strikes down the nations. He treads the winepress of God's wrath and bears the title "King of kings and Lord of lords" (19:16).

As Christ appears, an angel summons the birds of the air for the "great supper of God" (v. 17)—a grim counterpart to the marriage feast. Kings, generals, and mighty men become a feast for judgment—similar language found in Ezek 32:3-8; 39:17-20; and Isa 18:3-6. The beast and false prophet—symbols of false religion and corrupt government—are captured and thrown into the lake of fire, showing their final and irreversible defeat. The governments and armies of the world fall, not by human strength, but by the sword from Christ's mouth.

The Binding of Satan and the First Resurrection

John then sees an angel come down from heaven, holding a key and a great chain. The angel seizes Satan, binds him for a thousand years, and locks him in the abyss so he can no longer deceive the nations. This begins the millennium—a time when those who were martyred and those who remained faithful to Christ are raised to life. This is the first resurrection, and they reign with Christ for a thousand years. This reign reflects God's original purpose in creation—his people ruling with him, just as Adam was meant to rule under God's authority in Eden.

The "thousand years" should be understood the way Revelation often uses numbers—symbolically, not mathematically. Just as seven represents fullness and 144,000 stands for God's people and completeness, so a thousand here marks the fullness of God's appointed reign. It does not necessarily mean a literal 365,000 days, but it does point to a long and complete period of time set by God's design. Yet calling the number symbolic does not make the event unreal. The reign itself is real: Christ truly returns, the saints truly share in the first resurrection, and they truly reign with him for the full measure of God's purpose. John uses a symbolic number to describe a literal reality—the vindication and reign of the risen Christ with his people until the final resurrection and judgment (For further discussion on the millennial reign, please refer to the next chapter).

Why This Matters

This vision lifts our eyes to the certainty of Christ's victory. The marriage supper of the Lamb assures believers that history is not spiraling aimlessly but moving toward a joyful union of Christ with his redeemed people. It reminds us that the pleasures and powers of the world—like Babylon's counterfeit feast—are temporary and hollow, but the feast of the Lamb is eternal and true.

Christ's return as the Faithful and True Rider anchors our hope in his power to set all things right. Evil's reign will not last forever; every false system, every corrupt ruler, every source of injustice will bow before him. The same Savior who welcomes his Bride in love is also the righteous Judge who brings justice to the world. This gives courage to persevere in faith, knowing that salvation and judgment are in the hands of the One who is both King of kings and Lord of lords.

The Return and Reign of Christ

But his reign means even more—it restores what humanity lost in Eden. In the beginning, Adam and Eve were created to reign under God's authority, stewarding his creation in perfect harmony with him. Sin fractured that calling, bringing death, sorrow, and separation. When Christ returns and rules with those who share in the first resurrection, he restores humanity's intended purpose: to reign with God in righteousness, peace, and joy. His kingdom fulfills the promise of a redeemed creation where the redeemed share in his victory and exercise the holy dominion first entrusted in Eden.

The Word of their Testimony

One of the leaders overseeing a network of churches has been arrested three times for his ministry work. On one occasion, someone inside the group turned out to be reporting information to the authorities. After his arrest, he was threatened and told never to continue this kind of ministry again. But he did not stop. Despite pressure, surveillance, and betrayal, he continues to lead and serve with boldness and wisdom. Endurance often means carrying the weight of leadership under threat—and doing it anyway.

Questions for Reflection and Discussion

- How does the contrast between Babylon's fallen banquet and the marriage supper of the Lamb challenge what we value and pursue in this world?
- Christ's robe is dipped in blood before the battle begins (Rev 19:13). What does this reveal about the source of his victory, and how does it deepen your view of the cross?
- The certainty of Christ's final victory over evil can feel distant. How can this promised future reign give you courage and hope in the struggles you face right now?

CHAPTER THIRTEEN

The Release of Satan and Final Rebellion

What John Sees

AFTER THE MILLENNIUM REIGN of Christ, Satan is released for a final rebellion but is swiftly defeated and thrown into the lake of fire. Then John sees the great white throne judgment.
Reference: Revelation chapter 20:7–15

Gog, Magog, and the Final Rebellion

After the saints reign with Christ for a thousand years, Satan is released—and immediately resumes his ancient mission: to deceive the nations and rally them for one last war against God and his people. His nature hasn't changed; restraint never reforms him. John identifies these rebellious nations as "Gog and Magog" (20:8), deliberately invoking the prophetic imagery of Ezek 38–39.

In Ezekiel's vision, Gog is the chief prince of Meshech and Tubal, gathering distant nations to attack God's people. This follows Ezek 37, where God resurrects his people from the valley of dry bones, breathes life into them, and places them under the rule

The Release of Satan and Final Rebellion

of the one Shepherd, the Messiah. The sequence is unmistakable: resurrection → restoration → rebellion → judgment → lasting peace.

John's vision mirrors that pattern. First comes the resurrection of the saints—those who reign with Christ during the millennium (Rev 20:4–6). Then, after a thousand years, Satan is released, Gog and Magog rise, and the final rebellion unfolds. God answers with decisive judgment, followed by eternal peace in the new creation. But this raises crucial questions: If the first resurrection includes only the righteous, who are the nations Satan deceives at the end? Are these mortals who somehow survived Christ's return? Could the saints themselves fall in the final hour?

To answer that, we need to ask one of the most debated questions in Christian theology: What is the millennium? For centuries, believers have wrestled with whether the thousand years in Rev 20 should be taken as a symbolic description of Christ's present reign (amillennialism) or as a literal reign on earth following his return (premillennialism). Much of this debate turns on whether Rev 19 and 20 describe a single sequence of events or two parallel visions of the same climactic battle.[1]

Amillennial interpreters teach that Satan was bound at the cross and that his power to deceive has been greatly restrained ever since. They understand the first resurrection either as the believer's new birth in Christ or as the believer's entrance into heaven at death. A strength of this view is that it highlights the victory of Christ's death and resurrection as something believers experience now. They root this in passages like John 12:31, Col 2:15, and Rev 12:9–11, which emphasize that Satan's rule has already been broken. This view also upholds the unity of Christ's return, teaching that both the righteous and the unrighteous will be raised together for judgment in one climactic event (John 5:28–29; Acts 24:15). Yet problems remain. Revelation 20 says Satan was bound "so that he might not deceive the nations any longer" (Rev 20:3), and the New Testament confirms that Satan is the one who blinds the eyes of people (2 Cor 4:4). It's not until this reign and the end of Revelation that his deceiving is stopped, yet history shows as well that

---

1. Schreiner, *Revelation*, 659–82.

nations have continued to be deceived throughout the current age. Also, the picture of the saints reigning with Christ for a thousand years seems hard to reconcile with a purely heavenly reign, rather than the earthly rule described in the text. Amillennialism views chapters 19 and 20 as one parallel vision—two accounts of the same final battle. It rightly recognizes their shared themes: cosmic conflict, rebellion, and divine victory. But the text makes careful distinctions. In chapter 19, the beast and false prophet are destroyed, while Satan isn't dealt with until chapter 20. The story unfolds in stages: first, the defeat of beastly powers; then a period of peace as saints reign with Christ; and finally, Satan's release and defeat, followed by final judgment. Parallelism helps us see the unity of the vision, but it doesn't erase its sequence. John isn't merging chapters 19 and 20 into one event—he's showing that Christ's victory happens in ordered steps: his return, the resurrection and reign of the saints, the brief rebellion, and the final judgment.

Premillennial interpreters believe the thousand years describe Christ's literal reign on earth after his return. They take the first resurrection as a bodily resurrection of the righteous who reign with him, and the second resurrection as that of the unrighteous for judgment after the millennium. This view's strength lies in its straightforward reading of Rev 20: it sees two resurrections separated by a literal thousand years. It also allows for a literal fulfillment of Old Testament promises, like those in Isa 65:17–25, which describe long life, peace, and prosperity in a renewed world where death still exists but is limited.

But serious questions arise. If Christ's return brings final victory, why is Satan released again to lead another rebellion? How could mortal people survive Christ's judgment and continue to live and die during this time? Most importantly, if Rev 19 already describes the total defeat of the beast and the kings of the earth, who remains alive to be deceived when Satan is released? This is the problem of the nations. Scripture gives no indication that survivors remain after Christ's final appearing. The New Testament consistently teaches that his return brings total judgment, not partial renewal, and an end to death itself (2 Pet 3:10–13; 1 Cor 15).

The Release of Satan and Final Rebellion

To propose that some people survive into the millennium creates tension with the broader witness of Scripture and introduces theological challenges that the premillennial view struggles to resolve. Furthermore, the New Testament consistently presents history in terms of only two ages, the present age and the age to come. A post-resurrection "middle" age in Revelation that resembles the present age appears foreign to this framework and seems difficult to reconcile with the rest of the New Testament's vision of redemptive history.

Ezekiel helps unlock this puzzle regarding the millennial reign. In chapter 32, he paints a vivid picture of many nations already in the grave—Assyria, Elam, Meshech, Tubal, Edom, the princes of the north, and the Sidonians. These aren't living empires; they are defeated enemies counted among the dead. Ezekiel calls it Sheol; John uses the Greek term Hades—but both refer to the realm of the dead. Later, in chapters 38–39, Ezekiel gathers all these names under one banner: Gog of the land of Magog. This name becomes a symbol of all the nations that ever opposed God and were judged by him. John picks up this pattern in Rev 20. When he says Gog and Magog rise again, he isn't describing a living empire—he's describing the resurrection of the unrighteous dead, all of God's enemies gathering one final time in rebellion after the saints have been raised and reigned with Christ.

The reference to the north deepens the symbolism. In Hebrew thought, *ṣāfôn*, translated as "north," was both a literal direction and a symbol of cosmic threat.[2] Jeremiah 1:14–15 describes disaster from the north. Isaiah 14 and Ezek 32 place the kings of the north in Sheol. To Ezekiel's audience, the north represented both historical invaders and spiritual forces of death and rebellion. So, when Gog and Magog come "from the north," the image goes beyond geography. John follows the same pattern in Rev 20 but makes its meaning clearer: "And they marched up over the broad plain of the earth and surrounded the camp of the saints and the beloved city, but fire came down from heaven and consumed them" (v. 9), revealing that Ezekiel's localized invasion was

---

2. Bible Hub, "6828. tsaphon."

always pointing to a global resurrection of the unsaved. This gives us a crucial insight: Gog and Magog are not surviving nations or saints who turn in rebellion—they represent the totality of human hostility against God, raised for final judgment. These are those who rejected God in life and persist in their defiance even beyond death.

Then John sees the vision of the great white throne. The unrighteous dead stand before God. The books are opened—one recording every deed, the other, the Book of Life. The sea, death, and Hades give up their dead. No one escapes. Death itself is cast into the lake of fire, along with all whose names are not found in the Book. This vision ties directly back to Rev 20:4–5, where John distinguishes the first resurrection (the saints) from the rest of the dead who "do not live again" until the thousand years are over. These are the nations deceived by Satan—the unrighteous dead, raised to rebel, and judged in the end.[3]

John gives us two perspectives on the same event: Gog and Magog as corporate judgment, the great white throne as individual judgment. From a limited human perspective, these may appear as a sequence. From heaven's vantage point, they may be one climactic act of justice.

Gog and Magog stand as the ultimate symbol of rebellion, just as Babylon symbolized the worldly empire. Babylon represents corrupt systems throughout history. Gog and Magog represent hardened rebellion at the end of history. Both are destroyed. No rival remains. What Ezekiel foresaw—nations buried in disgrace—John brings to completion. The enemies of God rise one last time, only to meet their end. And the people of God enter everlasting peace.

Why It Still Matters Today

This reading offers a compelling solution to the long-standing debate over the millennium. It presents the return of Christ as

---

3. Schreiner, *Revelation*, 659–82.

The Release of Satan and Final Rebellion

comprehensive, final, and universal. The first resurrection belongs to the righteous; the second, to the unrighteous. Their uprising reveals the persistence of evil. Their defeat confirms the finality of God's judgment. And Satan is silenced—no longer able to deceive. From that moment forward, rebellion is gone forever. The story that began with exile from Eden ends with homecoming in the new creation. The Lamb reigns. His people reign with him. Evil is finished. The victory is complete.

Theologically, the Gog and Magog vision affirms two truths. First, judgment is not arbitrary—it reveals the depth of willful rejection. Gog and Magog rise only to expose what was always true: those "whose names are not written in the Book of Life" (20:15) have chosen separation from God. Second, salvation is wholly of grace. Even in resurrection, when confronted with the unveiled glory of God, the wicked remain unrepentant. They rise—not to worship—but to make war. In the end, the Gog and Magog vision unmasks the human heart apart from Christ: hostile, unrepentant, and set against God. This theme echoes throughout the New Testament, where humanity apart from Christ is consistently portrayed as opposed to God (Rom 8:7; Jas 4:4).

Questions for Reflection and Discussion

- How does the pattern in Ezekiel (resurrection → restoration → rebellion → judgment → peace) help clarify the meaning of Rev 20?
- How does this reading offer a solution to the millennium debate?
- What does the rebellion of Gog and Magog teach us about the unchanging nature of evil and the justice of God's judgment?
- In what ways does this vision of final victory encourage the church today to endure suffering and remain faithful?

CHAPTER FOURTEEN

The New Creation

What John Sees

THE FINAL FULFILLMENT OF God's promise is unveiled: a new heaven, a new earth, and the new Jerusalem where God dwells with his redeemed people in perfect holiness and joy. The curse is gone, the Lamb reigns, and eternity begins in a world made new.

Reference: Revelation chapters 21—22:5

A New Heaven and a New Earth

After the defeat of Satan and the final judgment of the dead in Rev 20, John is given one last, breathtaking vision—not of destruction, but of eternity's beginning. These final two chapters unveil the climax of God's redemptive plan: a new heaven, a new earth, and the new Jerusalem where God dwells with his people forever. This is not mere symbolism—it is the full unveiling of what God promised from Genesis onward.

John sees "a new heaven and a new earth, for the first heaven and the first earth had passed away" (21:1). This is not a mere renovation of the old order but a completely renewed creation, free from death, decay, and sin. The sea is no more, symbolizing the removal of chaos, separation, and fear. At the center is the

The New Creation

new Jerusalem, descending like a bride adorned for her husband. This city is not only a place but a people. God dwells fully with his people: "He will dwell with them, and they will be his people" (v. 3) The covenant promise spoken through the ages now finds its ultimate fulfillment. From the throne, God declares, "Behold, I am making all things new" (v. 5). Death, mourning, crying, and pain are gone forever, replaced by life unending in his presence.

The New Jerusalem: God's Dwelling

John is shown the new Jerusalem in radiant detail. The city's perfect cube shape mirrors the holy of holies in the temple, signifying that God's full presence, once confined, now fills the entire creation. The foundations are adorned with precious stones, and the gates bear the names of the tribes and apostles—Old and New Covenant united, one people of God forever. There is no temple in this city, "for its temple is the Lord God the Almighty and the Lamb" (v. 22). John sees Ezekiel's visionary temple (Ezek 40–48) as fulfilled in the Father and Jesus. The symbol has given way to reality. The city needs no sun or moon, for the glory of God illuminates it, and the Lamb himself is its lamp. The gates are never shut, for there is no night and no threat. Nations and kings bring their glory into the city—not to exalt themselves, but to worship Christ, fulfilling Isaiah's vision of restored Zion in chapter 60. Culture and diversity are not erased but glorified, woven into the fabric of worship.

Yet holiness defines the city: "Nothing unclean will ever enter it . . . but only those written in the Lamb's book of life" (Rev 21:27). The redeemed walk in, but sin and rebellion are forever excluded.

Understanding the Two "Outsides"

Zechariah had already pictured this division when he warned that nations refusing to worship the King at the Feast of Booths would be left without rain and under plague (Zech 14:19). John takes that imagery and expands it, showing two distinct kinds of "outsides" in the new creation.

First are the redeemed nations, who dwell in the new earth and enter the city's open gates to worship (Rev 21:24–26). Their "outside" is spatial, not moral—they live in the new creation but return again and again to the holy city. Zechariah pictured this same reality when he wrote of the nations "going up year after year" to keep the Feast of Booths (Zech 14:16). His warning that Egypt and other nations would suffer punishment if they refused to go up (Zech 14:19) anticipates the separation of the "second outside" John describes.

The second "outside" is moral and eternal. The unclean, the unbelieving, and the immoral remain excluded forever (Rev 22:15). Their outside is not beyond the gates—it is the "second death" (21:8), eternal separation from God. What Zechariah expressed in covenant curse language—no rain, plague, exclusion from blessing—John expresses in new-creation terms: being left outside the city, cut off from the water and tree of life. Both prophets make the same point. Those who worship the King enter his blessing; those who resist remain under curse and exclusion.

The River and the Tree

John sees a "river of the water of life flowing from the throne of God and the Lamb" (22:1). On either side is "the tree of life, bearing fruit in every season and bringing healing to the nations" (v. 2). Eden is restored, but more than restored—it's remade. The curse is lifted, the tree is accessible, and God's people reign with him forever. They see his face, bear his name, and live in unending fellowship with their Redeemer.

A Living Kingdom

The new Jerusalem is the throne of God's presence, but not the totality of the new creation. Beyond the city, the new earth stretches

The New Creation

outward, reflecting his glory in resurrected cultures and redeemed nations. The story moves from a garden to a city, from exile to homecoming, from scattered peoples to a unified kingdom. God's people dwell in God's place under God's rule—forever.

Why It Still Matters Today

The final vision of Revelation is not an abstract future fantasy; it is a present source of hope, identity, and perseverance for God's people. John's glimpse of a renewed creation—where God dwells with his redeemed people and the curse is gone—shapes the way we live now.

In a world marked by grief, injustice, and death, this vision assures us that pain and loss do not have the final word. The promise that God will wipe away every tear and that death shall be no more speaks directly to persecuted Christians and to anyone enduring hardship today. The certainty of a coming world free from sorrow strengthens us to endure faithfully in the present. The new Jerusalem also shows that God's ultimate desire has always been to dwell with his people. Even now—before the city descends—believers experience a foretaste of this reality through the indwelling Holy Spirit. This vision calls the church to live as a holy dwelling of God today, anticipating the day when his presence will fill all creation. We endure suffering with courage, resist the seductions of Babylon, and invite the world to drink freely of the water of life, because our future home is secure, our King is near, and his kingdom will fill the earth.

THE WORD OF THEIR TESTIMONY

One man, once deeply committed to another faith, encountered the word of God and everything changed. What had once seemed unshakable crumbled in the light of the gospel. Now he not only follows Christ but is actively discipling others. His transformation reminds us that no heart is unreachable, and that the gospel remains the power of God for salvation to all who believe.

Questions for Reflection and Discussion

- What does the image of the new Jerusalem as a bride teach us about the covenantal relationship between Christ and his church?
- How does the absence of a temple reshape our understanding of God's presence in eternity?
- Why is it important that the tree of life reappears at the end of the story?
- What does this say about God's plan from Genesis to Revelation?

CHAPTER FIFTEEN

Jesus Is Coming

What John Sees

John sees and worships the angel delivering the revelation, but he is corrected and told to worship only God. The angel speaks on behalf of Jesus until the Lord Himself interrupts and speaks directly. He declares that He is the Morning Star and that He is coming.
Reference: Revelation chapter 22:6–21

Worship God Alone

JOHN'S FINAL VISION INCLUDES a humbling scene: "I fell down to worship at the feet of the angel but he said, 'You must not do that! I am a fellow servant. . . . Worship God" (22:8–9). Even the apostle who had walked with Jesus was so overwhelmed by the vision's glory that he instinctively bowed to the angel. The angel quickly redirected him: worship belongs only to God.

This moment teaches two vital truths. First, only God is worthy of worship. Angels, no matter how radiant, are still created servants alongside the prophets and all who keep God's word. The command "Worship God" draws a sharp line between Creator and creature; glory belongs to the Father and to the Lamb on the throne. Second, messengers speak with the authority of the Sender but are never the object of worship. Throughout Scripture, angels and prophets sometimes speak as if in God's own voice (e.g., Exod 3; Judg 2). This reflects the ancient custom of a king's herald: a royal messenger could proclaim, "Hear ye! The king says . . ."—speaking in the king's voice, yet remaining only a servant. In Rev 22, the angel functions as that herald—delivering Christ's words with his authority—yet refuses worship because he is not the King. When Jesus himself begins speaking in verse 12, the distinction becomes clear: Christ is no herald but the divine King who alone deserves worship. This rebuke guards the church from two errors—idolizing angels or treating Christ as merely another messenger—and directs our focus to the One seated on the throne and to the Lamb who was slain.

Do Not Seal the Prophecy

The angel tells John: "Do not seal up the words of this prophecy, for the time is near. Let the evildoer still do evil . . . and the holy still be holy" (vv. 10–11). This command contrasts sharply with what the prophet Daniel was told centuries earlier: "Seal up the words . . . for it refers to the time of the end" (Dan 12:4, 9). Daniel's visions pointed far ahead, so the scroll was to be kept for a later generation. John's vision, however, is not for a distant future but for the present age of the church—an age already living in the last days between Christ's first and second coming.

The statement "the time is near" emphasizes that the decisive events of God's kingdom have already begun in Jesus's death, resurrection, and ascension. The church must therefore hear, obey, and proclaim Revelation now; it is not a sealed mystery waiting for some far-off era.

The next line—"Let the evildoer still do evil . . . and the holy still be holy"—does not endorse sin or indifference. It underscores the urgency and finality of choice: God's word demands a response. As history moves toward Christ's return, people's hearts become fixed in their chosen paths—those hardened in rebellion grow worse, and those who belong to Christ grow in righteousness and holiness.

In short, while Daniel's sealed scroll awaited the distant "time of the end," John's open book declares that the end has already begun in Christ, and the call to repent and be faithful is immediate. The church cannot afford delay; we are summoned to keep these words, proclaim them boldly, and live as those set apart for the coming King.

The Root of David and the Morning Star

The climax of Revelation is not merely the city, the river, or the tree but Christ himself. After unveiling the splendor of the new creation, Jesus makes a personal declaration that draws all attention to him: "I am the root and the offspring of David" (Rev 22:16). With these words, he reminds the church that he is both the origin of David's line as the eternal Son of God and the descendant of David as the promised Messiah who came in the flesh. He is the source and the fulfillment of every covenant promise.

Then he adds, "the bright morning star." Earlier, in his letter to the church in Thyatira, Jesus promised to give the morning star to those who overcome (2:28). Now, at the story's end, he unveils the full meaning of that promise: the reward for the faithful is not a thing but a person—Jesus himself. He is the morning star.

Jesus is the true reward of the faithful and the center of all history and hope—the Lamb who was slain yet stands in victory, the King of kings who rides forth in righteousness, the Alpha and the Omega, the Bridegroom, and the Bright Morning Star.

The morning star appears in the darkest hour before dawn, announcing that the night is almost over and the day is about to break. For the church that clung to Christ's promise through tribulation and darkness, this image is profoundly personal: the One who sustained them in their suffering now shines as their everlasting light. The Morning Star heralds the end of the night and the arrival of the eternal day.

All of Revelation leads to this: Jesus—the Bright Morning Star—our inheritance, our crown, and our everlasting joy.

Guard the Prophecy

John closes the book with a solemn warning: "If anyone adds to these words, God will add to him the plagues described . . . and if anyone takes away, God will take away his share in the tree of life and in the holy city" (22:18-19). This is one of the strongest cautions in all of Scripture. It underscores the holiness and finality of God's word. Revelation is not a human story that can be edited, softened, or expanded at will; it is the unveiled testimony of Jesus Christ given to his church. Adding to the prophecy would distort God's message—altering his promises, his warnings, or his plan of redemption. Taking away would diminish the hope and the holiness that the book holds out to the faithful. Both actions are treated as rebellion against the Author of Scripture himself.

The severity of the penalty—losing access to the tree of life and the holy city—shows that tampering with God's word is not a minor offense but a direct challenge to his authority and truth. The same God who spoke creation into existence and who seals his covenant promises also protects the integrity of his word to the very end of the Bible.

The Final Invitation

The Bible ends not with fear but with invitation. "The Spirit and the Bride say, 'Come!' And let the one who hears say, 'Come!' Let the one who is thirsty come; let the one who desires take the water of life without price" (22:17). Jesus himself speaks: "Surely I am coming soon." And the church replies, "Amen. Come, Lord Jesus" (v. 20).

The close of Revelation is not about escaping this broken world but about entering the joy of a world made new—a renewed creation where righteousness dwells, tears are wiped away, and life flows from the throne of God. The final invitation centers everything on a Person, not a place: Jesus is the reward. He is the living water for the thirsty soul, the Bridegroom who welcomes his people home, and the One who promises, "I am coming."

Questions for Reflection and Discussion

- What does it mean that Jesus is the Morning Star?
- In what ways is Christ himself the ultimate reward of the faithful, beyond crowns, cities, or kingdoms?
- How does the final invitation ("Come!") shape our mission and hope in the present?

EPILOGUE

Jesus, the Morning Star

THE STORY OF REVELATION is not a code to be cracked but a testimony to be trusted. It begins with a persecuted church, struggling to remain faithful in a hostile world, and ends with a victorious Bride, radiant in the glory of her Lord. Along the way, seals are broken, trumpets are sounded, bowls are poured out, and beasts rise in defiance. Empires fall, Babylon collapses, and Satan rages. Yet through every vision, one truth holds steady: the Lamb reigns.

Revelation does not promise escape from tribulation, but endurance in the midst of it. The saints are called to overcome—not by power, compromise, or violence, but by the blood of the Lamb and the word of their testimony. The church suffers, but it does not fall. Evil surges, but it does not prevail. God's people are sealed, secured, and carried through.

The judgments of God are sobering but never arbitrary. Trumpets warn, bowls finalize, and the great white throne settles every account. The unrighteous dead, resurrected in the second resurrection, march in final rebellion only to be consumed by God's fire. Their uprising reveals the hardened state of the human heart apart from grace. Judgment is just, because rebellion persists even in the face of glory.

But judgment is not the last word. The last word is life. The last vision is not wrath but renewal—not a world ending in ashes, but a creation remade in beauty. The new Jerusalem descends. The river flows. The tree of life heals. The curse is gone. God's dwelling is with his people. The throne is in the midst of them, and they see his face. What was lost in Eden is not merely restored—it is surpassed.

And at the center of it all is Jesus. He is the Lamb slain yet standing, the King of kings who rides forth in righteousness, the Alpha and the Omega, the Bridegroom, and the Bright Morning Star. To the church in Thyatira, he promised the Morning Star as a reward for faithfulness (2:28). At the end, he declares, "I am the Bright Morning Star" (22:16). The promise was not of something but of Someone. The reward is himself.

This is the great hope of the church: not simply a city, a crown, or a kingdom—but Christ. He is our inheritance, our light, our life, and our joy. He is the end of night and the dawn of unending day. He is the answer to every prayer, the fulfillment of every covenant, and the completion of every longing.

And so, the Bible ends not with fear but with invitation. "The Spirit and the Bride say, 'Come!' And let the one who is thirsty come; let the one who desires take the water of life without price" (v. 17). Jesus responds: "Surely I am coming soon." And the church, with all her hope fixed on him, answers: "Amen. Come, Lord Jesus" (v. 20).

Until that day, the church endures. She suffers, but she sings. She groans, but she hopes. She resists compromise, proclaims the gospel, and lifts her eyes to the One who is coming. Revelation closes the canon of Scripture with the assurance that history is not spiraling into chaos but marching toward consummation. Christ will return. Evil will be defeated. Death will end. And the Morning Star will rise forever.

Glossary

The 10/40 Window

"The box or 'window' that runs from northern Africa, the Middle East and Asia between 10° north and 40° north of the equator. The 10/40 Window has a few specific difficulties that missionaries and churches have to take into consideration. Many countries in this area are hostile to Christianity and hinder its momentum. Every believer can be subjected to hostility from family members, governmental agencies, and other individuals or organizations in the area. Because of this, missionaries and funding to advance Christianity in these areas are often scarce. Jesus has called all Christians to take this hope everywhere, even to the most challenging places in the world."[1]

The 1,260 Days/42 Months/Time, Times, and Half a Time

A prophetic time period found in Daniel and Revelation (Dan 7:25; 12:7, 11–13; Rev 11:2–3; 12:6, 14; 13:5), expressed in three ways: 1,260 days, 42 months, and time, times, and half a time—each representing the same span of three and a half years. This began as a literal period during the Maccabean revolt, when the temple was desecrated and daily sacrifices ceased. Yet this literal span became a symbolic pattern of ongoing tribulation. It was prophetically initiated in the Maccabean era, advanced through the destruction of the temple in AD 70, and continues through the

---

1. 10/40 Hope, www.1040hope.org, paras. 1, 3.

Glossary

gentile domination of Jerusalem until Christ returns. Throughout this time the church suffers, bears witness, and remains faithful in the face of opposition.

Abomination of Desolation

A prophetic phrase from Daniel and referenced by Jesus to describe a defiling act directly related to the temple that brings judgment.

Antichrist

A term describing both a spirit of deception already active in the world and a final figure who will embody that rebellion before Christ returns. John teaches that "many antichrists" have already come (1 John 2:18–22; 4:3; 2 John 1:7), identifying the antichrist as a recurring force working through those who deny Jesus. Paul refers to "the man of lawlessness" (2 Thess 2:3–8) not just as one person but as a representative title, culminating in a final individual who will gather all previous opposition into one last rebellion, only to be destroyed at the coming of Christ.

Antiochus Epiphanes

A Seleucid king who ruled from 175 to 164 BC and violently persecuted the Jewish people. He outlawed Jewish worship, defiled the temple by sacrificing pigs on the altar, and erected an image of Zeus inside the sanctuary—an act known as the abomination of desolation (Dan 11:31). His actions fulfilled Daniel's prophecy in a literal and immediate sense, but also serve as a foreshadowing of future tribulation, including the desecration seen in the destruction of the temple in AD 70 and the spiritual rebellion that continues until Christ's return. Antiochus stands as a prophetic type of the antichrist—a ruler who exalts himself against God and persecutes his people.

Glossary

Apocalyptic

From the Greek *apokalupsis*, meaning "unveiling" or "revelation."[2] It refers to a literary genre marked by symbolic visions, cosmic imagery, and divine messages delivered through angels or dreams. Typically written during times of crisis or persecution, apocalyptic literature reveals hidden spiritual realities and the ultimate triumph of God over evil. The book of Revelation fits this genre. It doesn't just predict future events—it pulls back the curtain on the spiritual dimension of current and future history, offering hope and assurance to believers that God remains in control despite outward chaos.

Armageddon

The prophesied location of the final battle between the nations and the returning Christ. Mentioned in Rev 16:16, Armageddon is not just symbolic—it marks a real, climactic confrontation where the kings of the earth unite to make war against the Lord and his saints (Rev 19:19). This event is foretold in Ps 2, Joel 3, Zech 14, and Jude 14–15, where God gathers rebellious nations for judgment. Christ defeats them by the word of his mouth, bringing the reign of evil to an end and establishing his kingdom in glory.

Babylon

Symbol of the world's corrupt systems—political, religious, and economic—that oppose God. In Rev 17–18, Babylon is portrayed as seductive and powerful but ultimately judged and destroyed.

Beast

Revelation 13 introduces two beasts: one from the sea (symbolizing political power) and one from the earth (symbolizing false

---

2. Bible Hub, "602. apokalupsis."

religion). Both are empowered by Satan and oppose Christ and his people.

Book of Life

The heavenly record of those who belong to Christ. Those whose names are written in the Book of Life are spared from final judgment (Rev 20:12-15).

Covenant

God's binding promise to redeem and dwell with his people. Revelation reveals the fulfillment of this covenant through Christ's victory, judgment, and the new Jerusalem.

Gog and Magog

Figures from Ezek 38-39, symbolizing a final rebellion against God. In Rev 20, they represent the unrighteous dead raised to oppose Christ one last time before final judgment.

Great White Throne

The final judgment scene in Rev 20:11-15, where the dead are raised and judged according to their works. This event follows the second resurrection—the raising of the unrighteous, whose names are not found in the Book of Life. The righteous were already raised in the first resurrection to reign with Christ (Rev 20:4-6). Now, the rest of the dead—those who rejected God—stand before the throne and are judged. Death, Hades, and all who remain in rebellion are thrown into the lake of fire, the second death.

Glossary

Maccabean Revolt

A Jewish uprising in the second century BC (167–160 BC) against the Seleucid Empire and King Antiochus IV Epiphanes, who had desecrated the temple in Jerusalem by outlawing Jewish worship and erecting pagan altars. Led by Judas Maccabeus and his brothers, the revolt successfully reclaimed and rededicated the temple. The revolt is historically significant and prophetically important, as the events—especially the 1,260 days of temple desecration—served as a literal fulfillment of Daniel's prophecy and a symbolic pattern for future tribulation leading up to Christ's return.

Messiah

The Anointed One promised in the Old Testament and fulfilled in Jesus Christ. Revelation shows the Messiah as the slain Lamb, the victorious Rider, and the reigning King of kings.

Millennium

The thousand years described in Rev 20:1–6, during which the resurrected saints reign with Christ. Though the number is symbolic, it points to a real and extended period of Christ's victorious rule after his return. During this time, Satan is bound, the faithful share in Christ's authority, and the earth begins to experience restoration. The millennium anticipates the new creation and restores what was lost in Eden, as righteousness, peace, and justice begin to reign.

New Jerusalem

The holy city described in Rev 21–22, where God dwells with his redeemed people forever. It represents the fulfillment of all God's promises—a world made new.

Glossary

Persecuted Church

Christians around the world who suffer for their faith. Revelation offers them assurance, calling them to endure and promising ultimate vindication.

Resurrection (First and Second)

The first resurrection refers to the raising of the righteous to reign with Christ (Rev 20:4–6). The second resurrection includes the unrighteous dead, who are raised for judgment at the great white throne (Rev 20:12–15).

Seals, Trumpets, Bowls

Three escalating cycles of judgment in Revelation. The seals (Rev 6–8) begin to unfold after Christ's ascension, representing the troubles and tribulations leading up to his return. The trumpets (Rev 8–11) come later at the final seal, intensifying the warning as the end draws near. The bowls (Rev 15–16) are poured out at the very end, with the last trumpet, unleashing God's final wrath as Christ returns with his people in victory.

Sheol/Hades

Biblical terms for the realm of the dead—Sheol in Hebrew (Old Testament) and Hades in Greek (New Testament). Both describe the temporary state before final resurrection and judgment.

Thlipsis (Tribulation)

A Greek word meaning "crushing pressure" or intense affliction.[3] In the New Testament, it describes the suffering experienced by faithful believers in a hostile world. John uses this word in Rev 1:9,

---

3. Bible Hub, "2347. thlipsis."

identifying himself as a fellow partaker in the tribulation, along with the churches he writes to. This tribulation is not reserved for the future but is already present, marking the church's ongoing struggle to remain faithful in the face of opposition.

Titus of Rome

A Roman general (later emperor) who led the destruction of Jerusalem and the Second Temple in AD 70 during the First Jewish-Roman War. Under his command, Roman legions breached the city, burned the temple, and ended the sacrificial system—an event seen as fulfillment of Jesus's prophecy in Matt 24 and Luke 21. Titus's actions echoed the abomination of desolation first seen under Antiochus Epiphanes and advanced Daniel's prophecy of the sanctuary being destroyed and the daily sacrifice ending (Dan 9:26–27). This marked a key stage in the ongoing period of desolation and gentile domination that will continue until the return of Christ.

Witnesses (Two Witnesses)

Figures from Rev 11 who represent faithful testimony in the face of opposition. They may be symbolic of the church or literal prophets in the end times—or both.

Wrath of God

God's holy and just response to sin and rebellion. In Revelation, his wrath is revealed in stages and poured out fully in the final judgments—distinct from the tribulation believers endure.

Bibliography

Bible Hub. "602. apokalupsis." https://biblehub.com/greek/602.htm.
———. "2347. thlipsis." https://biblehub.com/greek/2347.htm.
———. "6828. tsaphon." https://biblehub.com/strongs/hebrew/6828.htm.
Keener, Craig S. *Revelation*. NIV Application Commentary. Grand Rapids: Zondervan, 2000.
Schreiner, Thomas R. "New Creationism." In *Theistic Evolution: A Scientific, Philosophical, and Theological Critique*, edited by J. P. Moreland et al., 875–92. Wheaton, IL: Crossway, 2017.
———. *Revelation: The Hope of Glory*. Wheaton, IL: Crossway, 2022.
Walton, John H. *Genesis*. NIV Application Commentary. Grand Rapids: Zondervan, 2001. Kindle.

www.ingramcontent.com/pod-product-compliance
Lightning Source LLC
Chambersburg PA
CBHW072200100426
42738CB00011BA/2485